Who's Better Than You!

Who's Better Than You!

Who's Better Than You!

Who's Better Than You!

Vinny Vella
Life Stories

Gary D. Morgan

Who's Better Than You!

First Printing

Copyright © 2024 Gary D. Morgan

All rights reserved.

No portion of this book may be reproduced in any form without written permission from the publisher or author, except as permitted by U.S. copyright law. Written permission can be requested from: *Thewesleybarn@gmail.com*

For privacy reasons, some names, locations, and dates may have been changed, and incidents either are the products of the author's imagination or are used fictitiously. In some cases, resemblance to actual persons, living or dead, businesses, companies, events or locales is entirely coincidental.

Cover and Book Interior Designer: Roger Dapiran

Library of Congress Control Number 2024914943

ISBN Hardcover 979-8-99107-16-3-5

ISBN Paperback 979-8-9910716-1-1

ISBN E-Book 979-8-9910716-2-8

Printed in the United States of America

Webpage: *Heywhosbetterthanyou.com*

Email: *WhosBetterThanYou@yahoo.com*

"As long as I can make people laugh, tell stories, have my friends around me and my family.

Hey, who's better than me!"

–Vinny Vella

Who's Better Than You!

PHOTO CREDITS

Gary D. Morgan: Cover, Inside Flap, Back Cover, Pages XVI, 21, 31, 48, 102, 170, 183 and 204

Paul Borghese: XXXI-XXXV

Gary D. Morgan and Vinny Vella: XX

Adrian Vella: 196

Margaret Ann Vella: Pages XIV, 213 and 238

Vinny Vella: Pages: 2, and 125

ACKNOWLEDGMENTS

Thank you to Vinny Vella for his friendship, endless humor, and the great stories contained in this book.

Thank you to Margaret Ann Vella and Vinny Vella Jr. for their friendship and most valuable contributions to making this book a reality.

Thank you to my wife Deborah for her support and valuable input.

Thank you to my son David for his counsel and skills.

Thank you to Roger Dapiran for his serendipitous appearance to design and put this book together.

Thank you to Laverne Y Berry Esq. for her legal counsel.

Thank you to Paul Borghese for his compassion, commitment and dedication to making this book happen.

Thank you to Justine Pawlukewicz for her editing contributions.

Thank you to my family.

Thank you to Don Hughes for his support.

Thank you to Frank Lisi for his knowledge and assistance with the Italian language.

Who's Better Than You!

Thank you to Maria Giorgio for her knowledge and support.

Thank you to Erik Hoover who makes things happen.

Thank you to authors Keith Hedger, Rich Docherty and Linda Guecia for their contributions.

Thank you to all the celebrities who provided tributes to the book: Armand Assante, Vincent Pastore, Kathrine Narducci, Paul Borghese, Dominick Chianese, Anthony Michael Hall Jim Jarmusch, Michael Rispoli, Tony Darrow, Joe R. Gannascoli, Joe Causi, Michael Madsen, Gianni Russo, Barry Pepper, Al Sapienza, Joseph D'Onofrio, Tony Ray Rossi, Lauren Mascitti, Leo Rossi, Victor Colicchio, Louis Vanaria, William DeMeo, Artie Pasquale, Jackie Martling, John Huba, Peter Mazzeo, Michael Musto, Joseph Dinki, and Mike Lawler.

Table of Contents

My Vinny XV

Preface XVII

Introduction XXI

Tributes XXXVII

School Days 1

The Mission of the Immaculate
Virgin at Mount Loretto 5

Fooling Around 7

My Twin Brother 11

The Irish Girl 15

1953 MG Convertible 19

I'm a Lover 23

Otisville State Training School 25

Tony Pastor's 33

Rikers Island 41

The Matzo Ball 45

Who's Better Than You!

Greenwich Village 47

The Card Game 51

My Friend Enzo "How to Succeed" 53

On the Run to Florida 57

I'm on Vacation from a Vacation 63

Mr. Sinatra 69

My Father 75

Bellevue Psychiatric Hospital - Locked Up 81

New Orleans Lockup 91

Mom and the Eight Million Dollar
Lottery Ticket 97

Whatever You Do Don't Touch It,
They're Gonna Fix 103

What a Drag 107

Joe Rigano 109

I Just Won $5 Million in the Lottery 117

That's the Most Beautiful Girl I've Ever Seen 127

Cocaine and Clorox 135

You Trying to Make a Monkey Out of Me? 141

Casino 147

You Never Told Me You Were in *Spiderman* 153

We're All Look-Alikes 157

Nicknames 165

The Spanish Guy	169
My Wife	171
Don't Believe That Sick Bastard	175
The Little Person and Cold Steaks	179
Mausoleum Shopping Trip	181
La Bella Ferrara	183
Jokes	187
Marriage	191
No One Is Going to Screw Me	197
The Movie "Director"	199
San Gennaro Festival Ice Pick Accident	205
Have You Ever Had a Woman Like Me Before?	207
Good Thing I'm Vinny Vella	209
I Would Have Been Better Off Traveling to Jamaica, Queens	211
I Need a New Travel Agent	215
Margaret Ann Shares a Story	217
King Tut's Ring	219
Margaret Ann's Favorite Vinny Vella Credits	233
Who's Better Than You	235
Epilogue	239
Afterword	241

Who's Better Than You!

MY VINNY

It's been nearly 40 years since we met, believe it or not. We met at a Catholic school dance and instantly fell in love or lust and from that night on we were never apart.

Vinny was a guy that most people when meeting him either loved or hated him. Myself, I loved him.

The hardest thing I've had to do was learn how to live without him. I consider myself privileged because I remember all of Vinny's stories.

What I remember is enjoying the reaction from anyone listening to his stories.

I hope you find his stories of love and chance and humor enjoyable as well.

- Margaret Ann Vella

Who's Better Than You!

XVI

PREFACE

Vinny Vella of *Casino* and *Sopranos* fame saw it all and delighted in telling everyone he encountered about his life, his adventures, and his acting career. Vinny in story after story regales the reader with the deeds and misdeeds of his life.

Born in Greenwich Village, Vinny grew up in a family with three brothers and three sisters. His dad earned enough money as a bicycle racer at the Madison Square Garden Velodrome to afford to open up a fish store in Little Italy.

From his youngest days in grade school, Vinny describes himself as "Not a bad kid, just a very mischievous one." Thrown out of four grade schools for various infractions of which he may or may not have been guilty, Vinny tells hilarious stories of blaming his "twin brother" for many of the predicaments he found himself in. Vinny ever the survivor rallies the reader to hysterical laughter and tears with stories of his motorbike accident, lottery ticket misfortunes, an encounter with Hobo The Chimp, numerous chance meetings with Frank

Who's Better Than You!

Sinatra, his Rikers Island vacation, matzo ball soup, Miami Beach in the 1960s, haphazard meetings with shady characters, Little Italy situations, King Tut's ring and show business insider stories. Let's not forget about the girls!

People from all walks of life and all ages will identify with his stories. You don't have to be Italian or a New Yorker to enjoy his chronicles. Come take a peek into the hilarious antics of a life that contained a series of remarkable events.

It was my good fortune to have met Vinny for the first time at La Scatolina Restaurant located on the Avenue of the Americas and 9th Street in Greenwich Village. It was at an actor's networking event in 2009. I immediately felt his presence as he held court over those gathered, talking about the acting business and his many life adventures both in and out of the business.

In 2012 we sat down weekly, taping his life stories at La Mela Ristorante on Mulberry Street. My intention was to transcribe and fashion his stories into a book.

We would habitually venture over to La Bella Ferrara after lunch to have a cappuccino at an outside table. Vinny would routinely be recognized and be asked to sign autographs. I took pictures of Vinny with anyone who handed me a camera and asked me to take a picture of them with Vinny. Vinny loved engaging with everyone who stopped by to speak with him.

Preface

I have heard the stories contained in this book a thousand times over. They are universal. Vinny never tired of entertaining those around him. We would engage with his good friends Nick and Frank the owners of La Bella Ferrara and the laughter was non-stop. I was fortunate to meet many of Vinny's long-time friends who would often stop by to chat.

Vinny was a natural storyteller serving up stories that had everyone laughing no matter how many times you heard the story. I, for one, never tired of hearing the stories and laughed at his takes on life, which were unique.

It occurred to me that his ability to relate his stories to everyone he encountered would make a great one-man show. We worked on putting the show together for approximately seven months. In September of 2012, Vinny performed the first of four sold-out shows at The Duplex, a world-renowned historic venue in Greenwich Village that helped launch the careers of Woody Allen, Barbara Streisand, and Joan Rivers among many others. Performances followed at The Bitter End, Governors Comedy Club, and other venues.

In the meantime, I had the privilege of meeting Vinny's wife Margaret Ann, and son Vincent Jr., with whom I have relied to help assemble this book. Their love and affection for Vinny is contained within the covers of the book. They are both wonderful people who are stars in their own right.

Who's Better Than You!

The stories contained in this book are all fiction, unless they are true, and bear no resemblance to any real or fictional characters or persons. Names have been changed to protect both the innocent and the guilty.

I have attempted to remain true to Vinny's true character by relating the stories with only very minor adjustments for clarity.

I hope that this book is an enduring legacy of Vinny's life and the contributions to the happiness that he brought to everyone who enjoyed his performances, and the people he met along the way.

Vinny and the Author outside Albanese Meats and Poultry on Elizabeth Street.

INTRODUCTION

ONE OF A KIND

Believe it or not, I first met Vinny Vella in the mid-1990's on a set we both were doing what we called at the time, "featured extra work" aka background and stand-in work when we were just trying to keep busy in-between bigger gigs, to help make ends meet, and to qualify for our Screen Actors Guild health benefits. We just hit it off right off the bat and spent that first "hurry up and wait" working day together talking about anything and everything and boy did he make me laugh that day until my sides split! We immediately became tight from that point on. We were both living in New York City and chasing the dream. To show how hard this industry is, we were both accepting some of that sort of lower totem pole type work after Vinny had already played one of if not the biggest roles of his career as Artie Piscano in Martin Scorsese's *Casino*. But as Vinny would say to me back then, "You gotta do what you gotta do my boy." And we did. A handful of those smaller gigs took place before things really started taking off for us. It was around 1998 when we did our last gig of that kind for good! To this day I can still hear his voice and see that distinct little end of sentence mouth snarl to the side he would do. It was his trademark. There's no better way to describe it if you didn't know Vinny and don't know what I'm talking about, is that it most resembled my Nonno when he'd make a little motion with the side of his mouth to get something out of his teeth, or to adjust his dentures. If you know, you know. Just one of many little endearing quirks and qualities there were to being Vinny Vella.

I was married at the time (1995) to Malika Kinison and she and Vinny hit it off as well. The first time we all spent time together; Vinny, his wife Margaret Ann, Malika and I, she said to me, "Where did you find this guy, I love him!" From that day on there wasn't a time he'd talk to me on the phone that he wouldn't ask about her by saying, "How is the baby?" He loved our little Miniature Pincher, "Prancer" and he'd also ask, "And how is the little rug rat?" We literally talked on the phone every day. Vinny used to make his rounds so to speak, first by phone in the mornings and then by foot in the afternoon walking through Little Italy like he was the Mayor of it. Everyone knew Vinny, everyone yelled, "Hey Vinny" just as the documentary by John Hubba was titled. I lived on Bleecker Street at the time and Vinny on Elizabeth Street, both down-

One of Kind

town, so we often started our days by meeting at a little greasy spoon in Little Italy called BUFFA'S CAFÉ'. We were friends with the owner John, and I still am to this day. I fondly recall how Vinny would make me go to a bodega with him on those mornings before we'd go for our cheap but plentiful bacon, eggs, sausage and home fries breakfast; to pick up scratch off lottery tickets that he'd get right to it with a nickel as soon as we'd sit at our favorite table. If he won something, he treated for breakfast. If he didn't, I did. There were other times that the gum snapping waitress Darlene would come over at the end of our meal and say, "It's on John today".

In the fall of 1998 Vinny inadvertently got me my first feature film directorial gig by initially recommending me to play a role in the infamous Richard Castellano's *Four Deadly Reasons*. It was the same year that I was voted President of the then Italian Actors Union of which I renamed and reinvented as GIAA, the Guild of Italian American Actors and I appointed Vinny to my advisory board along with other Italian American actor friends of ours that joined the union once I was elected. The first actor I got to sign on was James Gandolfini during the first season of The *Sopranos* because I knew that other actors would follow if I got him onboard. Jimmy and I became friends when he took over my apartment on Bleecker Street and my wife and I moved to the top floor Penthouse apartment.

Who's Better Than You!

My wife at the time, Malika, was our VP. We slowly grew, with Vinny's help, and by us all spreading the good word. A fading union of only 67 members because there wasn't any Italian speaking theater in New York anymore, grew to over 500 members in the 4 years I was president. I will forever serve as President Emeritus although the union has dwindled since we all left office. Membership is sadly down to less than it was when we took over in '98.

So getting back to the fall of 1998. Vinny invited myself and a bunch of other GIAA actors up to Narrowsburg, NY for a barbecue at the late Richard Castellano's house in the Catskill Mountains for him to meet us and consider us all for roles in this movie he wanted to produce. Being more than just an actor and having producing and directing experience, I listened carefully and realized this guy didn't have a script that could be produced for the low budget that he wanted to produce it for; didn't have a good director of photography attached, or a director yet. That being said, Vinny gave me the eye, and at some point, got everyone to leave, and left myself and Malika there. The two of us continued talking to Richie and his wife Jocelyne about his film. Once he realized I knew what I was talking about, he not only cast both myself and my wife in roles but hired me to re-write the script with my long time buddy and collaborator, the renowned poet Joe

One of a Kind

Dinki who I chose to be my writing partner on this project. He then had me hire a Cinematographer and he and his wife Jocelyne offered the director position to me because I had a documentary film entered into their Narrowsburg Film Festival at the time that they loved and won awards there; *The Canadian Ballet*. It happened so fast and Vinny was ecstatic. He played one of the leads, "Slick" Sally, I wrote him the role. We filmed the trailer in March of 1999 with a lot of our actor friends like the late Joseph Rigano and Paulie Cicero, also Carmine Surace, Michael Belisario, Frankie Bonsangue, Sal Piro, etc., in order to create something for Richie to show his investors to raise the rest of the money to make the film. But after that weekend shoot we never thought the movie would ever get made, and the trailer footage we filmed was never edited. Then out of nowhere Vinny and I get the call from Richie that he has the money and he wants to shoot the movie that summer! Well we jumped all over it and as unorganized and crazy as Richie was, Vinny, myself, his wife Margaret Ann, my wife, and the rest of the cast had the best time over those two weeks we filmed up there all staying at an old Catskill Mountains B&B resort called Eddy's Farm. Every night we'd gather on the front porch of the old mansion and Vinny would tell us ghost stories. And I mean really good ghost stories that would scare the shit out of most of us, even as grown men.

Who's Better Than You!

Then he set up actress and cast member Lisa Regina to hide behind a tree with a white sheet over her and run through the woods as he was telling a scary story and I can't tell you how close people came to crying in fear before they laughed until they cried. He was a master of telling stories. I must have heard him tell the stories in this book a thousand times and I never got tired of hearing them. He was just like the Pied Piper leading us. The most flattering thing anyone could have said to me on set for that production was what Vinny said to me after the first day of production which was, "Hey Borghese... Scorsese WHO?!" Richie Castellano ran out of money toward the end of the shoot so Vinny and I found a way to get the movie finished with the help of my co-writer Joe Dinki who then became a producer on the film.

We brought other name actors in for the additional few days of filming like Leo Rossi and *Four Deadly Reasons* went on to have its premiere on opening night of the Tribeca Film Festival back in 2002. But not because it was an official entrée, but because Vinny and I came up with this great scheme to try to book the Tribeca Screening Room above the Tribeca Grill that Robert DeNiro owned, before they started scheduling the venues for the festival screenings. It was genius! With deposit on account, they couldn't cancel the booking so we set up our own little red carpet outside of the entrance, put a poster of the

One of a Kind

movie on an easel out front and all of our guests entered thinking they were attending a film screening on opening night of the inaugural Tribeca Film Festival which in actuality they were, just no one not even the passerby or paparazzi, knew otherwise. We did actually go on to screen at and win awards at quite a few other major film festivals. I hope to stream it soon so that many people who never saw the film can view it and see Vinny back then in the early 2000's.

We worked on so many other projects together after that, too many to even mention or remember but just to name a few so you can look them up to see more of Vinny's work: *Once Upon A Time in Brooklyn, The Irishman, Find Me Guilty, The Bakery, Analyze This, High Times Potluck, The Sopranos, Law & Order,* the TV pilots *From Geek to Guido, YOU GOT WHACKED; Gangsters and Pranksters* and the documentaries *BEYOND WISEGUYS: Italian Americans & the Movies* and *Narrowsburg*. Vinny was a prankster and one of my favorite pranks of his was when he'd call an actor friend of ours and impersonate an agent or casting director's voice and tell the actor that there's a role he has for him that he wants to book him on but he has to come to the office right away with all these different outfits to do a fitting for the director so the excited actor would gather up at least one full wardrobe bag of outfit options wanting to impress the agent or casting director as to how quickly he responded and how prepared he'd show up and when he'd get to the office they would tell the actor they had no idea what he was talking about. Stanley Kaplan was the agent who Vinny used to imitate for the prank calls and the casting director was Ricardo Bertoni. You will read about two of these pranks in the Joe Rigano chapter. I can't tell you how many actors fell for this prank! It was hysterical to be with and hear Vinny do Ricardo's accent so perfectly and sell the actor on it being a real deal call. After a while, once word got out about the prank, when the call would come in actors would call him out on it and say, "Velllllla?!" Just too funny!

I remember Vinny falling asleep and snoring while they were filming on Sidney Lumet's set when we worked on *Find Me Guilty* together. It was literally an almost dead silence courtroom moment when we all hear a rolling snore, and Sidney yelled, "CUT! – what the hell was that?!" And we all died laughing knowing it was Vinny. Even Sidney laughed. He also did that on another well-known Hollywood Director's set whose name I won't mention, but since he was only an extra on that one this particular crazy director kicked him off the set but not so much for that, but mostly because Vinny walked in on him in his personal bathroom while snorting coke, as a production assistant was doing something to him that she

One of a Kind

shouldn't have been doing. At least that's how the story goes. When I think of Vinny I can visualize his face as if I last saw him alive and in person yesterday. I can distinctly hear his voice and his laugh will never leave me. I picture those loose white pants he used to wear with the string tie in the front. Vinny would somehow get the wardrobe girl on every shoot he was on to let him keep his outfit so I vividly can picture Vinny's whole wardrobe. Always colorful yet casual, and he had his one or two dress up suits you'd see him in from time to time but he absolutely hated wearing a tie so he seldom did. I remember the day he married Margaret Ann. It was at a beautiful ballroom that adjoined a restaurant called 1050 because it was on the corner of 10th Avenue and 50th Street and a quaint hotel adjoined both. I knew the owner at the time and helped set it up. Both he and Margaret Ann looked like such a handsome couple and they were so happy. The funny part of the evening was when I saw a guy leaning against the wall not even in a suit and I thought it was this Robert DeNiro impersonator Joe Manuela that used to hang around and thinking Vinny may have invited him I walked over to say hello to him and was gonna break his balls about not getting dressed up more for the occasion but when I reached him to say hello, I realized it actually was Robert DeNiro. It was so interesting that he strolled into the reception late like that, completely un-

Who's Better Than You!

noticed except for by me, and I didn't even think it was him. Of course Vinny had invited him but it was so big of Bobby to show up like that to show his love and support of Vinny. Vinny's son Vinny, Jr. had also played Bob's son in *Analyze This*, so they got close through that experience. Instead of Vinny allowing Bob to just blend in, of course he had to make it a grand event out of him showing up so poor Bob got swamped when Vinny grabbed the DJ's mic and announced that "Robert DeNiro was in the house!" After things calmed down, Bob and his guest spent the rest of the night seated at the dais table with Vinny and Margaret Ann.

Vinny was a people magnet. There were some that he didn't like but for good reasons and there's always going to be someone that doesn't like you whether for a good reason or not, but general consensus would have to be that Vinny Vella was liked, loved, admired and respected by pretty much anyone that knew him.

. - Paul Borghese, Actor/Director/Producer

One of a Kind

On the set of *Four Deadly Reasons* (1999)
"The first movie I ever directed that Vinny had a lead in
and had told all his ghost stories to all of us every night
on the front porch of The Catskill Mountains
old hotel resort Eddys Farm.

Who's Better Than You!

Vinny and I on the set of *Delilah Rose* that we both played roles in. With our director Ric Pantale.

Me and Vinny

One of a Kind

Vinny and I with my cousin, Tony Darrow,
at an appearance event in Naples, Florida.

At the premiere of a faith-based movie
that I played the lead in, *Vito Bonafacci*.

Who's Better Than You!

Me and Vinny in Little Italy on Mulberry Street.

One of a Kind

On January 12th, 2018 I took Vinny out for dinner for his birthday to his favorite Italian restaurant DaNico in his neighborhood,

Who's Better Than You!

TRIBUTES

"I had been in touch with Vinny about the possibility of our working together and quite sadly, not so long before he passed away in 2019. Vinny was a life force whose extraordinary street and survival demeanor defined him both as a man but as well as an Actor. In Italian Theatre Vinny Vella is straight out of Commedia dell'Arte, a combination of Arlecchino and Pulcinella, and Un Vero Napolitano. He is a Lesson in the Improvisational Attitude that sustains the absurdity of our lives, and a reminder to laugh at ourselves, especially today when there's little left to laugh about." — *Armand Assante, Actor*

"Working with Vinny Vella on *The Wiseguy Show* on Sirius Radio was a blast and the many films we worked on together were great... But my best memory of Vella was in Toronto when we were working on different projects but staying at the same hotel. I asked Vinny, "so what's the movie about your doing" and he said, "I never read the scripts". That's an acting lesson from Vinny Vella." — *Vincent Pastore, Actor*

Who's Better Than You!

"I still have about 10 voice mail messages saved from Vinny that I will never delete. Some made me laugh out loud, some were really, really sweet. Some he was busting my balls as usual. It's hard for me to listen to them because I really miss Vinny a lot and I still can't believe he's gone. It's hard for me to visit Elizabeth Street because his memory is so embedded in me. I lived around the corner from Vinny on Mott street. Me, Vinny and Margaret Ann's whole family would sit in front of the building for hours eating, laughing, the kids having a ball. They actually had a little swimming pool that little Vinny would swim in and big Vinny would barbecue in the street. Vinny was probably one of the most funniest people and biggest Ballbreaker I have ever met in my life, I miss my friend dearly."

- Kathrine Narducci, Actress

"I knew Vinny because Vinny made a point of it to make sure that he knew everyone on every set he worked on, or every restaurant he ate in. I think he left an impact on everyone he met, including me." *- Dominick Chianese, Actor*

"That guy was a pisser! Paulie introduced me to him and there was an immediate comical connection we had. I think we laughed more than talked cause every other word out of his mouth had me cracking up!"

- Anthony Michael Hall, Actor, Producer

Tributes

"Vinny Vella was like family to me. For years we lived only a block away from each other, and he seemed to know everyone. Through Vinny I met a truly remarkable array of usual characters. I became friends with his close friend Joe Rigano, and of course his son Vinny Jr. and his wife Margaret Ann. Vinny appeared in several of my films and was always up for anything. A consummate storyteller, as this book will certify, I loved just hanging out with him or walking around the neighborhood observing his endlessly amusing interactions. My favorite of all his adventures might well be the one involving King Tut's ring— it is of course included here. Yeah, I miss Vinny. I don't like that he's gone. And I miss that monthly phone call, " Hey, Jimmy-boy, let's meet up for some French fries and coffee, whaddya say? How 'bout Cafe Habana — those cute waitresses over there really seem to like you too — you know, the ones with the tattoos and everything!" Ah Vinny, you're in my heart forever." - *Jim Jarmusch, Director*

"Vinny Vella was a big-hearted guy who could tell a story that would make me laugh 'til my sides hurt, then, as you were laughing, he would impart some poignant observation about the humanity of us all and it would bring me to tears. HE WAS THE WILL ROGERS OF ELIZABETH ST. He could draw you in with laughter and make you cry with his sage perspective. In that way, he was a very unique and generous soul. And he would often speak of his beloved Margaret-Ann with utter adoration. I say this, "God bless Vinny Vella, may our children sing of him." — *Michael Rispoli, Actor*

"My cousin Paul Borghese pretty much cast Vinny and I in every movie or TV show he directed so boy did we get used to working together and playing off of each other. Vinny and I had a natural comedic chemistry on and off camera. The laughs we had! He was quite the character, also both on and off camera. He is greatly missed by many." — *Tony Darrow, Actor/Comedian*

"Vinny Vella was an interesting guy, and a funny guy at that. He was always about trying to make people laugh and he always got a chuckle out of me when he'd be on the set of *The Sopranos*. It's sad to think that he's gone so long before his time. RIP Vinny." — *Joe R. Gannascoli, Actor/Chef*

"What can you say about a true New York original like Vinny Vella. He gave what the street taught him and delivered it in everything he did, both on the screen and in person. Probably one of most colorful characters you ever wanted to meet. As soon as you met Vinny he made you feel like family. After working with him many years on Sirius Satellite Radios *The Wiseguy Show*, which was the brainchild of *Soprano* actor and East Street Band musician Steven Van Zandt along with Vincent Pastore, Cha Cha, Joey Rigano & Uncle Floyd, Vinny Vella was always on point,

Tributes

always funny and one of the best guys to have in your corner. After a while he became more of a family member than a co-worker. I am so glad I had a chance to work and be friends with him."

- Joe Causi, Radio DJ, 101.1 WCBS FM

"That Vinny Vella, what can I say that hasn't been said."

- Michael Madsen, Actor

"Funny, funny guy, heart of gold. Always made me laugh."

- Gianni Russo, Actor, Carlo in the Godfather

"I'll never forget the time that Paul Borghese sent a limo to pick me up for an event he was being honored at and I shared the limo with Vinny and he made me laugh the whole way there and back until he ran out of steam on the way home and fell asleep on my shoulder and snored the rest of the way home".

- Barry Pepper, Actor

"Vinny Vella was a unique person and a very interesting actor. As much as he often did the same schtick, in some ways he never did the same thing twice. He was liked by many and loved by even more, and will be sorely missed."

- Al Sapienza, Actor

Who's Better Than You!

"Vinny was one of a kind. When he entered a room, he made everybody happy. He had a great personality and a big heart. Love him and miss him."   *- Joseph D'Onofrio, Actor*

"Vinny was charismatic. He was one of a kind. He was funny, clever and a true friend. He was generous. He never had a bad word to say about anybody. He would mesmerize you with his stories. You could have heard the stories 100 times and each time you thought it was a new story. He was Mr. New York."   *- Tony Ray Rossi, Actor/Hairdresser*

"I met Vinny through Paul Borghese and being an entertainer at the Blauvelt Sons of Italy Italian Feast in TAPPAN, NY for many years. I was so blessed to get to know Vinny when he would come and be a part of the festivities, Paul even honored him with a Lifetime Achievement Award. We would often ride to the airport in the same limo with him as they would drop him off at his home in the city and my Nana and I got to hear so many exciting, interesting and funny stories about his upbringing. He never failed to leave us in stitches! I even told him 'Vinny, you need to write a book!' My time with him was nothing compared to his family and the close friends that knew him and loved him, but even just getting to hang around him during the week of the festival every year was a blessing to us. His kind, sweet spirit just made you feel

Tributes

like a friend right away. Like he never met a stranger. He was such a precious, down-to-earth soul and he is sorely missed. We loved Vinny so much" — *Lauren Mascitti, Country Singer/Recording Artist, American Idol Finalist.*

"The first time I met Vinny was in Little Italy. I honest to God thought he was the Mayor! EVERYBODY knew him! He was a larger than life personality with a heart to match. As an actor Vinny was funny, talented and a pleasure to work with. He is missed" — *Leo Rossi, Actor*

"When Michael Imperioli and I were writing *Summer of Sam*, Vinny's scene in *Casino* was the inspiration for our dialogue. We wanted our dialogue to be as real and as truthful as Vinny's was in that movie. We could never figure out if his dialogue was scripted or improvised. We later found out it was a little bit of both. It was a real treat getting to finally meet him in 1999 on the set of Paul Borghese's directorial debut feature film, *Four Deadly Reasons* that both Vinny and I played roles in."
— *Victor Colicchio, Writer/Producer/Actor*

"I was a guest on Vinny's cable talk show once. Halfway through the interview I realized his life and personality was a lot more interesting than mine. I found myself asking HIM questions, and he always had the answers. LOL!"
— *Louis Vanaria, Actor*

Who's Better Than You!

"Vinny Vella, "Who's Better Than You", made everyone feel like there wasn't anyone better than themselves. He made everyone around him happy. Always smiling and always joking around. On the set of one of the movies I produced, *Wannabes*, he had me cracking up so much. Pure love for this man. God Bless!" - *William DeMeo, Actor/Producer*

"It's difficult to top " Whose Better Than You", but he certainly was unique. I sort of helped him with his stand up act but all I said was, just list and tell 3-4 experiences/stories (that only he knew how to tell), and he was a hit! He also was a charmer with the ladies although his love was his wife Margaret Ann. Miss him." - *Artie Pasquale, Actor*

"Talk about funny. This guy was put together with funny bones." - *Jackie Martling, Comedian*

"Vinny Vella was a rare talent whose presence both on and off the screen was nothing short of magnetic. I met Vinny as a young filmmaker and was overwhelmed by his charm and personality. I immediately knew that I had to make a movie about this larger-than-life character.

After hearing his stories for years, I hired a crew and began filming in and around New York City with his family and friends in what eventually became my first feature documen-

Tributes

tary, *Hey Vinny*.

I feel very fortunate to have become great friends with him during this process. His dedication to his craft, combined with his natural charisma, brought an authenticity and depth to every role he inhabited. Vinny's ability to connect with people was unparalleled; he had a unique gift for making everyone around him feel special."

*- John Huba, Photographer, Filmmaker,
Director* Hey Vinny

"I loved Vinny. I always looked forward to being in his company. His humor & personality were infectious. You couldn't help but laugh for hours& have great life conversations as well. He relished in the love of people being around him. He was truly a highlight in my life. God Bless you my friend."

*- Peter Mazzeo, Entertainer, Filmmaker,
Director* Life With Vinny

"Vinny was a real NY character and paisan. We had a blast working together on a local cable show called *New York Central*. He was fiery, funny and full of life and always wanted to take me to Arthur Avenue, saying we could hold out large shopping bags to be filled there. We never ended up

Who's Better Than You!

doing that--it sounded shady to me, lol--but I always enjoyed my Vinny encounters. And I also love this book, which vividly brings him and his lust for enjoyment back to life. Though I DON'T approve of the way he would throw bread rolls at drag queens he unknowingly made out with!!!"

- Michael Musto, Journalist

"Vinny was a natural talent; he lived the way he spoke: down to earth and very, very funny, joyful and inclusive."

- Joseph Dinki, Producer, Poet

"I go to the Italian feast in TAPPAN, NY every September and Vinny is like a fixture there. He was so embraced and loved by everyone there and was part of the entertainment even if not intended to be. He just stood out."

- Mike Lawler, Congressman

CHAPTER 1

SCHOOL DAYS

When I was a kid I wasn't a bad kid, I was just very mischievous. Parents used to tell their kids, "If I see you with that Vinny Vella you'll be grounded, and you won't go out," and to the girls, they said, "You'll never leave this house again." The fathers used to tell me "Vinny if I see you with my daughter, you're gonna have a problem.

Like I said I wasn't a bad kid."

I was suspended and thrown out of two parochial schools and two public schools for different reasons all of which I was innocent.

One of those schools was Our Lady of Pompeii School on Bleecker Street.

At one point my teacher sent us all down to the auditorium to take the school year picture. It wasn't a group shot; it was individual shots which they put together in a class shot. I was a little crazy back then.

Who's Better Than You!

So we went down to the auditorium. I got on line, took the picture, got off the line, combed my hair a little bit different, took my sweater off, got back online in a different pose, and took another picture.

So, when the photographer came about a month later and went over to my teacher Miss Bruno, he said, "Here is the picture of your fifty students." She goes, "Fifty, I only have forty-nine." He said, "You may have forty-nine now, but in here you have fifty pictures". She said, "Listen it's impossible, I've had forty-nine students for the past three years." He said, "I believe you, but in here you have fifty." She says, "It's impossible". Of course, she had forty-nine, until you see the picture.

School Picture Grade 5

School Days

I am on the upper right-hand corner on one side of the picture and I am on the lower left-hand corner on the other side of the picture. It took her about an hour to figure out that I was in the picture twice. So naturally, I got thrown out of school for that.

Another time in another school one day I decided it was time to end the school day. So, I told the teacher I had to go to the bathroom and instead I rang the fire alarm, ran downstairs, and rigged a fishing wire across the bottom of the stairs. Well, how would I know that one of the students would trip on the wire and break his leg and another kid would get a broken arm?

The nuns were always mean to me because I was a troublemaker. They used to hit me with hangers. One day in fourth or fifth grade I got caught with my hand under the desk. I had my hands in my pants. I might have been scratching myself or moving it around a little bit. This nun came over behind me and said, "What are you doing?" I took my hands out of my pants and said, "It's not what you think." She said, "You know you could go blind doing that." I said, "Sister don't worry about it. I'll do it till I need glasses."

I was always getting in trouble, between that and not wearing ties. I got thrown out of all the schools in my neighborhood. They were Our Lady of Pompeii, P.S. 3 on Hudson Street between Bedford and Grove Streets, P.S. 41 at 6th Ave and 10th Street, and St. Anthony's at Houston and Sullivan Streets.

Who's Better Than You!

CHAPTER 2

THE MISSION OF THE IMMACULATE VIRGIN AT MOUNT LORETTO

At that time I don't think there were many more schools in the neighborhood, so I was put up in boarding school. I was sent to Mt. Loretto in Staten Island. I was pretty bad at one point and I remember one morning I woke up and my father didn't go to work that day. I knew something was wrong. My mother and father told me at that time, they said, "We're going to bring you up to this place in Staten Island 'cause we were told by the courts that we had to show you this place in Staten Island, and that if you didn't behave, you would wind up there."

There was a priest, his name was Father Kenny, and when we entered the place they seemed to know who my mother and father was. They must have thought I didn't notice it, but I seen Father Kenny motioning to my mother. He motioned with his eyes and head and my mother and father got up as if they were ready to leave. I was getting up and he put his hand on my shoulder and he said, "Vincent stay here a minute because I want to speak to you." So I said, "But I want my mother and father here." And he says, "They're not going anywhere just stay here 'cause I want to speak to you." As my mother and father were leaving the office there was glass behind them which was like a hallway so I could see them walk by and as they were getting up to leave the office I noticed my father. Tears were coming from his eyes.

I knew something was wrong. I knew right there and then they were leaving and I waved to my father from the window. My mother didn't have a tear in her eyes. She pushed him into the car and that was it. I was left there. I got into a lot of trouble after that evening.

I noticed that each and every place I ended up in after that, Otisville, Rikers Island, etc. it was only my father that came to see me, not my mother. I miss my father so much. My kid will never see a bad day as long as I am around.

CHAPTER 3

FOOLING AROUND

Here I was. I don't remember how old I was, maybe nine, ten, eleven years old? My sister Cookie to get out of the house, she had to tell my mother she was taking me to the park, taking me somewhere. She would not let my sister out by herself, 'cause she was only fifteen or sixteen years old. So my sister used to take me out and bring me over to her girlfriend's house. She said, "You can't tell Mommy that I'm going to bring you here. She's a nice girl, she is a friend of mine. You know you could play games and all that other stuff with her." I didn't know what she meant by that. The girlfriend would babysit me so my sister could go out on her date. I just watched TV and played games. She was a pretty little thing with long black hair. I don't remember how old she was fourteen, fifteen, sixteen?

After I was in the house with her for a little bit we were sitting on the couch watching TV and then she just got up and stood in front of me and she goes, "What would you do if you ever seen me naked?" I was in shock. I never heard that before. I didn't know what the fuck to say. I said, "I don't know. I would do something. I don't know what I would do." So she went into the room and opened up her robe. It was the first time I ever looked at it and did it look beautiful. I didn't know what to do. Man, I was all excited, and I got a hard-on right away. Then the doorbell rang from downstairs. She buttoned up right away. She said, "Don't tell anyone what I just did. Let me answer the door and I'll talk to you later." I never touched her. I never did anything. Nothing happened.

I remember a week or two later I told my sister. I said, "When are you going to take me over to your friend's house so you can go out with your friend?" That was the first time and the last time. I never seen the girl after that. That was the first time I ever fell in love with a woman. I wanted to get to that right away, so I had women on my mind since that point. She lived on 12th Street between Sixth and Seventh Avenues and there were these three buildings that looked alike, identical buildings and I didn't remember which one it was, or what apartment because I would have gone back and rang the fuckin' bell.

The first time I ever got a little piece of ass I must have been around 14 years old. Her name was Fat A. The girl, that was my sister's friend, she was fat, and she always used to get around me and pinch me, in my building downstairs near the first floor,

Fooling Around

underneath the staircase and I used to pinch her back. She said," What are you afraid to touch me?" And I used to like, grind up against her and feel her tits and all that other shit.

    Still, I never got nothing at that point.

    I needed to get laid so bad.

Who's Better Than You!

CHAPTER 4

MY TWIN BROTHER

So, now, I used to rob parking meters when I was a kid since they were so easy to open. You just had to put a key in there, open the thing upwards, and pull the things out to empty out the dimes. Sometimes you would see those meter maids putting the money in their pocket and close it up. There was a rod and I used to knock it out with a little chisel. You pulled it and emptied the dimes out of the box and put the rod back in there. I had a little chisel, and a hammer, and then pulled the rod through the other side.

You know, I was 10 or 11 years old at that time.

So, there was this place on Sixth Avenue and West Third Street called Delvy's. It was a clothing store. So they had a leather jacket in there that I wanted. I had two pillowcases that I stole from my mother, and they were filled with dimes from the parking meters in my neighborhood which I robbed. She was looking for her pillowcases and I had them down in the basement filled with dimes.

So I went into the store, and I said to the guy, "How much is that leather jacket?" He wanted $49.95. I said, "How many dimes is in $49.95?" and he says, "Hey listen to me, there are 10 dimes to a dollar, go home and figure it out!"

So the next day I came back with $50 in dimes and got the coat.

So the word was out on the street that Vinny Vella was buying stuff with dimes.

All of a sudden, the next thing I hear is a knock on my door and I opened it up and I knew right away it was the cops. I seen two cops. Now remember the school picture. It was hung up in the apartment on the wall to the left when you walked into the apartment next to the door. As soon as you walked in the door that was the first thing you would see. The cop said, "Vinny Vella get up against the wall! Where is your mother and father?"

Now my mother and father were next door at my neighbor's house, but if I would have told them that, they would have gotten my mother and father out. I know that if I got caught, my mother she would have ratted me out in a friggin' heartbeat. My father was an angel. But my mother she was a rat, I'll be honest with you. She was a gestapo too.

So I said, "They went to Brooklyn, they went to go visit

My Twin Brother

my aunt and uncle." I said, "I'm not Vinny. You're not looking for me," I said, "You're looking for my twin brother." "What twin?" said the cop. I said, "See I'm Frank, you're looking for Vinny." The cop said, "What do you mean?" So I took the class picture off the wall pointed and showed them the two of us. I said, "Here's Frank, and here's Vinny." So one cop looks at the other and says, "Oh my God, there's friggin' two of them." I said, "What'd he do now?" He's always giving my mother and father a lot of trouble."

They were staring at the picture for a while. And so they says, "He was robbing parking meters." I said, "He just left, he's with his friend Enzo, he just went to McDougal Street. When you get him, lock him up, he always gives my mother and father lots of trouble". "We'll be back." "I am sure you will. Don't worry you'll get him; he just went there."

About four hours later they had me by the collar, on the street, dragging me home. I said, "I am Frank." The cop said, "Shut the fuck up."

So they brought me home and they knocked on the door. My mother opened the door and they said, "Mrs. Vella, Vinny or Frank? Now my mom who had a beautiful Italian accent said, "Vinny or a Frank? He's a Vinny! The cop said, "So where's his twin?" "Twin?" my mom says. "If I would have had two of him when he was born, I would have killed the two of them!" The cop

Who's Better Than You!

said, "Well he showed us a picture over there on the wall." My mom said, "Don't mind him he's a nuts, he's a screwed up in the head, he takes the golf balls." She meant goofballs. "He smoke a the funny cigarettes. He's a taking the picture two times. They threw him out of school for this. Take him away, he makin' me a lotta trouble".

They put me in the Spofford Youth House at 1220 Spofford Avenue in the Bronx. If you don't know much about Spofford, you need to know it was not a walk in the park. And I'll leave it there.

It didn't matter 'cause all my friends were there anyway.

CHAPTER 5

THE IRISH GIRL

I couldn't go out with any of the Italian girls in my neighborhood because the fathers used to tell me, "Vinny if I see you with my daughter, I'll break your legs and my daughter won't go out of the house till she's 50 years old!"

Seventh Avenue was a borderline. You had the Irish on one side and the Italians on the other side. You didn't cross over but well…

I was going out with this Irish girl in my neighborhood. Her name was Leena. I'm about thirteen years old. So I lifted my hand and touched her breast, and she gave me my first smack in my face I ever got from a girl. A week later her brother chased me down the street with a machete. Then later I figured out these Irish, they're crazy. The Italians are looking to put me in the box and the Irish want to kill me with a machete. But he never caught me.

About a month later I see her on the street, and I says, "Hey you're Leena." She says, "You'd better stay away from me

Vinny Vella!" I said, "No, no, no, no, don't get me confused. You were going out with my brother." "What do you mean by your brother?" "My twin brother, " I said. "What twin"? she said. So I said, "You went out with Vinny, I'm Frank." She goes, "Wait a second, hold on a second." I said, "You went out with Vinny, I'm Frank." She goes, "Wait a second, hold on a second, you're Vinny!"

So I says, "I can prove it to you. Come with me." I can tell you she came with me but she kept her distance. I says, "I'm not Vinny, stay here right now, let me go upstairs." I got the school picture and came downstairs and I showed it to her and said "Here I am over here and here's Vinny. He never told you that he had a twin?" Leena said, "He never told me that." I said, "He broke up with you?" She said, "He didn't break up with me, I broke up with him!" "What did he do?" "He touched me." "You know what, he's always been a real asshole." "What did he do when he touched you?" "Well you know he touched my breast and if my brother gets him, he'll kill him." I said, "He's been like that with all his girlfriends, really disrespectful. If you were my girlfriend that would have never happened. That's why he never told you anything about me 'cause I'm totally different when it comes to things like that." She started to say something like "I can't believe that, I mean…" So, as I'm talking to her, all my friends are passing

The Irish Girl

by and saying, "Hey Vinny, hey Vinny." So I said to her, "You see that's how identical I am. They all think I'm Vinny all the time." She said, " I don't believe this, he never told me." I said, "You know if I would have been able to go out with you that would never have happened. Is there any way you and I could go to a movie or something like that?" She looked at me, thought for a few seconds, and said, " I guess so, that would be okay."

I decided I needed to go back to the movies so I could show her what a good guy I was. So now later on, when I was kissing her, she said to me "You even kiss the same way as him." And I said, "You see that's how identical we are."

Luckily, she moved out of the neighborhood about a month later. They all moved to Jersey, the whole family, but I had her fooled.

That's when I realized. You know what, I'm good if I could fool her, I'm a good actor, I got a gift there, I got the gift of gab.

Who's Better Than You!

CHAPTER 6

1953 MG CONVERTIBLE

I stole a car on Jones Street in Greenwich Village between Sixth and Seventh Avenue. It was a 1953 MG convertible. Nice little car.

That's how I learned how to drive. Back then if somebody pulled into a spot and there was a lot of room in front of the car, you could push the car in the spot. You could put the car in gear. Back then cars were easy to start up. You just opened the hood. I don't remember how to do it now, but back then you could hotwire them. In those days a lot of cars, even the small cars, you could put them in neutral, get around the street, give them a nice push, and throw it in gear. They would start up. You didn't even need a key. People left their car doors open back then. Cars back then were so beautiful. I'm talking about the actual looks of the cars. Not like today you can get a Jaguar or you can get a Honda, they all look the same. The only ones that don't look the same are if you have a Bentley or a Rolls-Royce. Even the Rolls-Royce autos are starting to look like these Chrysler cars with the grill in the front. It's all fucked up. They don't know what they are doing no more. Back then a 53 Chevy or a 53 Triumph or an MG, all these cars had different looks, including Studebakers which they don't have no more.

So I was driving around the neighborhood in the 1953 MG. I went around where my father was in Little Italy, and I was coming down Mulberry Street from Hester Street and I was really like tearing ass down the street. And I'll never forget as I was tearing ass down the street a little kid came running out in the street, not into the middle, but I seen him coming out and I panicked 'cause I didn't want to hit him. So I turned the car to the left and I hit the curb and I went up on the sidewalk. There was a water hydrant. Not only did I knock down the water hydrant with all the water coming out, but I wound up on the steps of the building. The building is still there, and the water hydrant is still there. All the world's water came out sky-high.

I jumped out of the car, and I ran. Then I went home, and my father says, "Sonamabitch, where were you today?" I said, "I was home, I was around." He said, "You were in the car on a Mulberry Street, a little car. What car? Stop telling me what car. Five people see you getting out of the car, you make a the car go up on the sidewalk and then you run." He said, "Don't lie to me, people they know you like I know you; they see you. You know you lie. Why you do that?" I said, "Pa." He said,

1953 MG Convertible

"Look, you know what, I don't want to even talk about it no more." "Don't go to the neighborhood for at least a couple of weeks 'cause they a looking for you. Stay out of the neighborhood and if anybody asks you if that was you, say no."

All right, so I had to stay out of the neighborhood for a while. Everybody knew that it was me, even the cops. They never arrested me. They knew my father and all that.

The location of where the accident took place was on Mulberry Street between Grand Street and Hester Street

Possible location of the "crime."
Has the statute of limitations run out?

Who's Better Than You!

CHAPTER 7

I'M A LOVER

The first time I ever got laid it was a hooker. I told a friend of mine, "Listen man, I gotta get laid. I'm the horniest bastard, man."

I'm 14 or 15 years old and I met this girl and at that time it was like five dollars for a blow job, ten dollars to get laid. I brought her to a place. It was called the Broadway Central. It was on the corner of Broadway and 3rd Street. Later on, years later, the building collapsed and the hotel that was in it. Luckily nobody got killed.

I was in that hotel; it was five dollars a night for a hotel room. I went in there. I didn't know what to do so I just laid on top of the girl. I just didn't know what to do. I didn't know you were supposed to put it in. I didn't know what the fuck to do. She said, "What are you doing?" I said, "Well…" She said, "Did you ever do this before?" "Not really", I said. "But I've seen somebody naked before." So she got me hard and then put it in her. Man that was like dynamite to me, I didn't know what the fuck was going on. It was like the fourth of July when that happened to me. I didn't know what the fuck to put it in. She was telling me what to do and she helped me.

Three days later my dick blew up. I went to pee and my dick was burning like a fuck and it started blowing up. It looked like a salami.

I had to go to the hospital to get a shot. The doctor gave me a shot in the ass. He called it the clap, syphilis and he gave me some cream and said, "Don't fuck around, don't do this, and don't do that for at least a week or two weeks." So that was my first time. So the doctor told me to use a Trojan. I said, "Does this happen every time when you fuck a girl without a bag?" He said, "You use a bag because you never know what these girls can have." He said, "Use a bag so this won't happen." I said okay to using the bag and I always used one ever since. After that first piece of ass, I just wanted it more and more.

At that time with all the girls I started going out with, I was just becoming like a lover, and I wanted to get into them right away and use the bag. I was like a champ from that day on, I was having a ball then.

No more hookers.

So now at that time, I'm starting to get it for nothing.

CHAPTER 8

OTISVILLE STATE TRAINING SCHOOL

Years ago when police officers went to the scene where a robbery was taking place or whatever, they would run there, and leave their engine running or shut the engine off and leave their doors open.

I was with Enzo on the street and the cops had stopped the car and ran into a building. So, all I wanted to do was sit behind the wheel and run the siren while they were gone and run the lights. I said to Enzo, "Come on let's get in the car." So we jumped in the car and turned on the lights. All of a sudden Enzo said, "Vinny! The cops are running towards us on both sides of the car." I threw the thing in drive, and I went on Morton Street and made the turn onto Bleecker Street. I got stuck in traffic after going 75 to 100 feet and end up being pulled over in front of Zito's Bakery. It so happened that I lived on that very corner at 272 Bleecker Street on top of John's Pizzeria. My windows faced Bleecker and Morton Street.

Who's Better Than You!

Well, because I was already on probation, I would be going up to upstate New York to the Otisville State Training School for Boys. Today it is a penitentiary. I was about 14 or 15 years old.

Back then it was a reform school. My sentence was for one to three years, and I did about 18 months. Enzo got on probation because he wasn't in any previous trouble before this.

Before I went upstate, they took me back to Spofford Youth House and the guys in reception recognized me. "Vinny you're back here. What did you do this time?" "They said I stole a police car." The cop said, "The record here says you actually stole it." "I didn't actually steal it. I just wanted to go for a little ride." The cop says, "You got balls man."

When I got upstate, they were all hicks up there. They segregated everybody up there. They put the gays in one spot, the troublemakers in another spot, and the kids that didn't do too bad in another area. So that's where they put me with the kids that weren't too bad.

There was this counselor Mr. H. He was a real redneck, and he did not like me at all. Every night when we got cigarettes from visitors, they would hold your cigarettes and put your name on the package of cigarettes and at night they would give them out like treats. They would give out either an apple, a cookie, or a cigarette. During the day they would give you a cigarette three or four times. At night I would wait for my cigarettes and Mr. H. would say "Vincent Vella" and I would say, "Here I am" and he would say "Vince Vella" and I would say "Here I am," and he'd do that two more times. I would say, "Here I am," and then he would go to the next guy. So, I said, "You called my name three times, here I am." He said, "What, are you answering me back? Get up against the wall with your arms out straight ahead and face the wall." He used to have me do that every night for an hour or more. Then he would mess up all the beds in the dorm and had me redo them all and clean the bathroom. He was just mean-spirited. If my arms went down a little bit, he'd come up behind me and smack me in the face, and he would continuously do that.

So one day I told my social worker about him. Then Mr. H. got me one night and said, "Hey you told your social worker. Listen, if you ever tell your social worker again, I'll beat your ass. You'll be making beds for the rest of the time that you are here." Every night he would take my cigarettes from me and not give me any cigarettes.

So, when the visitors came, my father used to bring cigarettes. I used to hide them outside 'cause we used to have to go out there and sit in the grass during the daytime. So, I used to hide them in a plastic bag underneath rocks and leaves under the tree and then I would light one up and smoke one out there because that bastard would not give me my cigarettes. I used to hold my own cigarettes. Me and my friends would be smoking at night and they would take one of my cigarettes and light it up so he wouldn't see me taking mine. There was Charles W. He thought I was one of the funniest guys he ever met and he would give me drags off his cigarette. He was a good guy.

At one point, Mr. H used to have me making beds every night and cleaning the bathrooms. He was just very, very mean to me. I would be the last one to get the mail or he would hold it for two or three days and then give it to me. He would smack me and smack me and smack me. I got to the point where I couldn't deal with it anymore. I spoke to this guy there named Eddie. I said, "One of these days he's going to smack me one too many times and I am going to kill this guy." Eddie used to be right behind me facing the other wall and I would be behind him facing the wall and he would turn around and check to see if my arms were going down or if I was leaning up against the wall. We used to help each other so that we wouldn't get caught.

So Mr. H smacked me one too many times and this one time I picked up a chair and hit him right in the back of the head. I opened up the back of his head. In every cottage, they had a panic button and if they pushed it the other guards would come from other cottages and break up whatever was happening. Mr. H was already out of play, he was out, and I got it from the guards who came in.

They threw me out of that cottage and put me in with all the nut jobs. The counselor I had in the cottage with all the nut jobs, his name was Mr. K. He was mean to me at first. I figured he would kick the shit out of me. The nut jobs were mean. They picked fights with everybody, and they really were troublemakers. They were kids that were continually walking around with attitude, and with chips on their shoulders saying, "Hey what are you looking at?" They would start fights with you for no reason, those were the bad kids.

I had to go to the Training School court a day or two later. They called it the "Kangaroo Court." When it was my turn to speak I said, "I complained to the social worker one time that my counselor Mr. H. kept always hitting me and hitting me and he continued to do it again and again." "Why did you hit him with the chair?" "Because he would continuously slap me." "Do you have proof?" I said, "Everyone in the cottage, they all seen what happened." So they went back there to the cottage and said, "Did anybody see him smacking me." They were all afraid to speak. I said, "Eddie please, and all of you, you gotta say something, you all seen him smacking me every night." They were afraid to talk. I said, "If you don't say anything they're going to hang me over here." I said, "Eddie, please say something." I said,

"Everybody is afraid to talk because they're afraid because he went to the hospital, and he had 14 stitches in the back of his head." I said, "Eddie please, everybody's afraid to talk." I said," If they talk will they be protected?" "Yes, they will." Eddie then said, "Yes he did", and he turned around to the rest of the cottage and everybody said, "Yeah it did happen."

I'll never forget it when I was put in the cottage with the nut jobs, Mr. K. said "Ah, you're the one that hit Mr. H". So I said to myself, you know what I have to stand up for who I am and what I did, because if not, it's going to happen over here too. I looked at him and said," Yeah I'm the one who hit Mr. H. and you want to know something, if anyone hits me again, they better not turn their back on me because you know what? The next one I'm going to kill." He said, "Get back inside with the rest of them." I was like the king of the cottage, and they labeled me like, "This guy's got balls." I was treated with respect from that day on.

My father was a good man. He was a hardworking man. He would come up and visit me every month. He had to wrap up things to give to them to check out and I told him to buy extra packs of cigarettes 'cause they were valuable. He always said, "Be a good boy so you can come home right away."

My mother was a real Gestapo. She had seven kids and my father married her when she was 16 years old, and she was

Otisville State Training School

probably so fucking upset that she had all these kids at such a young age that she always had a chip on her shoulder. I was the black sheep of the family. I am second from the baby, I had five older than me. I had two older brothers that were twins, they were Frankie and Louie.

I did 18 months and then I left.

Never seen Mr. H. again.

I lived at 272 Bleecker Street
on top of John's Pizzeria

Who's Better Than You!

CHAPTER 9

TONY PASTOR'S

McDougal Street in those days with Bob Dylan, Jimi Hendrix, and all the other musicians was quite a scene and everyone is doing acid, opium, hashish, cocaine, whatever, and pot.

I became 16 and I'm out on the street. I know this guy named Richie B. I used to look up to him all the time. I could use his name today, but back then I would not have been able to use his name 'cause I would have gotten in trouble. The reason why is because he was a numbers runner. Richie B. was a nickname he used. He was a guy from the neighborhood.

There was this spot on the corner of Sixth Avenue and West Third Street. It used to be a nightclub called Tony Pastor's at 130 West 3rd Street. It later became a McDonald's over there. All the wise guys used to hang out in that place. So one day he said, "Come on into the bar."

But first, let me tell you about him. Richie B. was 22 or 23 years old and always used to be dressed sharp, always had his nails manicured, and always wore suits with cuff links, and had a carnation on his jacket. He always had stacks of money and he had a babe on each arm. He was always groomed. He always looked like a million dollars. I always looked up to these guys. He used to say to me, "Hey don't hang out with those kids on McDougal Street. They're all taking drugs, you're gonna get in trouble, and I don't want you over there. Hang out over here with me. I'll tell you what life is all about." Before that, I used to hang out in the park when I was like 16, or 17 years old. At the time I looked 18 and could go into a bar, 'cause back then that's how old you had to be to drink.

He said, "Never get a tattoo from your elbow down because if you are ever wearing a short-sleeved shirt it makes you look like a punk. Always keep your nails nice and clean, always keep your hair nice, because if a girl sees you with dirty nails, they'll always say he's a bum." He said, "Keep your shoes nice and clean." Ever since then, I keep my nails clean, and my shoes shined. So, he said, "You got to change these clothes you're wearing. Meet me here tomorrow morning." So I met him the next day and he brought me for a haircut. He always seemed cool. He brought me for a manicure, and he even bought me a pair of shoes.

It reminds me of that movie *Goodfellas* where the kid came home, and the mother looked at him and said where did all this come from? He said, "I got paid for parking cars or whatever." So I said to my mom, "I got a job as a delivery boy." I didn't know what to say to her, I was running numbers. I couldn't tell her what I was doing. She says, "You sure? You don't sell any drugs, no?" I said, "Ma please, I don't sell drugs, I don't take that shit."

I was looking sharp so when I came home that day and my nails are all clean my mother says, "Where did you get all this a shit? Whaddya do with your fingernails?" I said, "My friend…" She said, "Whaddya mean your friend? You look like a sissy with your nails like this."

I had to keep my nails this way so the girls would see that I'm nice and clean. Later on, I had a little bit of money, so I got a cheap suit. I went to the flower shop and put a carnation on me. I wanted to be just like Richie B. You know what I did? I had about 30 or 40 dollars and I got all singles and I put them into a stack. I wanted to look like I had a stack of money back then. His was all these hundreds, fifties, and twenties and mine was all ones. I wanted to be a wannabe wise guy since I was a kid. It all started with Richie B.

I used to go to the bar at night and he said, "Hang out over here." One night I was leaving the club and he said, "Vinny, where are you going?" and I said, "Going home." He looked around and he said, "Here, do me a favor and take this envelope and drop it off at the social club up on Thompson Street." In the envelope were all these numbers. So, I put the envelope in my pants up front, on top of that thing over there, and he gave me 20 bucks. $20 back then, in the early sixties. that was a lot of money.

So I walked outside the club and the cops said, "Freeze!" and they pointed their guns at me. I said, "Oh shit!" and I put my hands up. They searched me. They must have spotted me inside. So the cops find the envelope. The cop says, "What's this?" I said, "I thought there was money in this. I was going to open it on the corner." "Where did you find it? I said, "I found it in the bar." They said, "Why didn't you give it to the bartender?" I said, "I don't like him."

The wind-up was I get arrested and spend the night in jail. In the morning, I went to court and when I went in front of the judge. The judge said, "Where did you get this?" I said, "Your Honor. I found it in the bar." So, he gave me 30 days suspended sentence.

That very same day, that same night I went back into the club again and Richie B. was there with all the guys, and they were all shying away from me. They said, "Did you say anything?" and I said, "If I had said anything you guys wouldn't have been here." "What happened?" I said, "They gave me 30 days suspended sentence." They said, "You said nothing, said nothing, you didn't say nothing! He didn't rat us out!" They were kissing me on my head, shaking my hand, and squeezing my cheek. They said, "Come on in and have a drink with us." Richie says, "Rita, take Vinny in the back and take care of him." That was nice. She was a fox.

I still had the $20 in my pocket. I hung out a bit, I had something to eat and then I get ready to leave and Richie says, "Where are you going now?" I said, "I am going home." He said, "Do me a favor and take this envelope and make sure this one gets there." I looked around and didn't see anybody. So I took the same kind of envelope put in my pants in the back this time, on top of my ass and I went outside. The cops were outside the bar again and they say, "Freeze!" and I said, "What are you guys doing out here?" I said, "What are you guys waiting for me at night?"

They searched me and found the envelope. So this cop says, "Where did you get this one, wise guy?" I said, "This one I found on the way out near the door on the floor." He said, "You're the one who always finds envelopes." I said, "Maybe I am lucky." "What's in the envelope?' " I don't know." He said, "You're in a lot of trouble." At the same time, they're bringing out Richie B. and all these guys in handcuffs, and they are looking at me with that look that says, you better keep your freakin' mouth shut.

Who's Better Than You!

So when I went to the Sixth Precinct that evening on Charles Street the arresting officer said, "You just got out this morning. When the judge sees you again, he's gonna throw the book at you. You're gonna end up doing two years upstate New York." I said, "Two years!" "If you won't tell us who gave you this envelope, you're going to end up doing two years." I thought, oh man if I had to tell them where I got this envelope from then I'm gonna be up shit's creek.

So there was a cop in there that used to like my sister. His name was Mike. So when he came in, he said, "Hey Vinny what are you doing here? What do you come in here every day for a soda?" I said, "The cop keeps arresting me." "For what?" "For an envelope." The arresting officer said to him, "He just got out this morning and he went back in there again". I said, "He keeps arresting me for a freaking envelope." Mike says, "Where do you get these envelopes?" I said, "I keep finding them in the bar." He said, "Vinny, look the judge is not gonna like this." I said, " I'm going up for two years." He said, "No, at the most you'll wind up doing six months." I said, "What for a freaking envelope?" Mike said, "What do you want a trophy for what you did?" "You violated your probation. Unless you talk, you know what's going to happen." I said, "Oh shit." I thought if I rat on these guys I'll have to move out of the neighborhood.

So I went to court in the morning and the judge looks at me and says to the prosecutor, "Why does he look familiar?" He says, "Your Honor he's that kid that was here yesterday who found an envelope." "Where did you find this one wise guy?" I said, "I found this envelope near the door, Your Honor." "What are you trying to make a mockery out of this court?" I said, "No. I found it on the floor."

This time the Assemblyman from my neighborhood came to court, my family came, my sister and her husband, and my father came, not my mother. My mother would have said, "Judge do me a favor, please take him and put him away." My father called everyone, so, they were all there to help me out. My priest even came and he said to me, "I'm going against my principles. You know I don't like ya. I am only doing it for your mother and your father."

The judge wanted to know who everyone was. So then the judge says, "Let me tell you something, you have everybody here with you today. Seems like you have a good family. You have the Minister from your Church and the Assemblyman from your neighborhood. I tell you what I'm going to do. I'm going to add on 30 days and if I ever see you again in this courtroom, I'm going to throw the book at you." He said, "What were you doing in there, you are only 17 years old." I said, " Your honor I had to go to the bathroom." The judge said, "Twice, you were arrested. The other night it was for the same thing." I said, "I had to go to the bathroom that time too. Oh, Your Honor, it will never happen again. Thank you. Next time I'll go home to go to the bathroom. You will never see me again, thank you so much." I turned around to go out.

As I turn to leave they're putting the handcuffs on me. I said, "What are you doing?" The cop said, "You have to do the 60 days." I said, "No he just gave me…" "No, he added on 30 days because you violated your probation. You have to do 60 days."

So the judge says, "Is there a problem?" I said, "Yeah they're putting handcuffs on me". He says, "You got to do 60 days." I said, "What for a freaking envelope?" He goes, "90 days!" "What are you giving me 90 days for?" He said, "You want to curse at me?" I said, "I'm sorry Your Honor. He got me nervous putting the cuffs on me." "You violated your probation and got 60 days and now since you cursed, now it's 90 days total."

I said, "Look I'm sorry can I do 60 days again? Could you take that cursing off of there?"

That was the end of that.

CHAPTER 10

RIKERS ISLAND

So now I have to go to Rikers Island.

Well just before I went up there guys were disappearing from my neighborhood, even Enzo. Enzo disappeared a few weeks before that. Enzo was five foot four or something like that and he used to love horses. We'd go up like to City Island and New Jersey to rent horses. All of a sudden he disappeared. I went back to his mother and said, "Ma where is Enzo?" And she goes, "Leave him alone he's in Jockey School with his uncle down in Florida." I said, "Can I call him up?" "No, no, no, leave him alone he is doing very good." Back then when kids were getting arrested parents never wanted to say where they were. So another two kids disappeared from the neighborhood Danny and Jimmy. So I went to their mother and said, "Angie where is Danny and Jimmy?" She said, "Leave them alone. They're working in East Pepperell, Massachusetts. They're working with their grandfather on a lumber farm." "Can I call them up?" "Oh no, no, no! Leave them alone, they're doing very good.

Who's Better Than You!

So when I went to Rikers I hear people yelling "Vinny, Vinny." These people were telling me their son was in Jockey School, they're on a lumber farm. I couldn't understand this. So when Enzo's mom Gina came to visit her son in Rikers Island I said, "Gina when you go back to the neighborhood tell everyone I'm in Jockey School with your son, you rat ya." Everybody from the neighborhood was up there. Everyone in the neighborhood was saying" My son is doing very good he's in Vegas, or he got a new job, this one's over here, that one's in Arizona, he went to Jersey he got married." Because back then when kids were getting arrested parents never wanted to say where their kids were locked up. They were all in Rikers Island yelling "Vinny, Vinny."

I was over there a couple of days and we had to go on a line to go and eat. We had to go on the line to the steam table with our tray. The guy is slapping food onto my dish. Now back then they were serving what they called pigtails and beans and I had never had that before. All of a sudden, I see this curly thing coming out from underneath the beans. It was a pigtail, and they throw the beans on top and I look at it and I took my hand away from that tray 'cause I was afraid of that damn thing. I didn't know what the hell it was. I didn't know if it was a freaking mouse underneath the beans or what. So I told the guy, "What is that?" And he said, "Man, motherfucker it's soul food man, didn't you ever have pigtails and beans before?" I said, "I don't eat that shit." He said, "What you want man, pisscetti?" I said, "It's not pisscetti, it's spaghetti you fuckin' imbecile ya. I don't want that shit; you people are used to eating that shit." "What do you mean us people, motherfucker?" One thing led to another, and he threw it at me and I threw it back at him. The next thing you know we're fighting and everyone is getting up in the mess hall. Then they tell me I caused a race riot.

Then they put me in the hole, "The Bing." I lost track of time after a couple of weeks, I had to do the rest of the days in the hole. So I never got to see any of my friends except for just a couple of days.

It was about a week or two later when I asked the guard "What time is it?" And he said, "What do you have a fucking date?" That answered my question. Every once in a while, I'd ask him, "How are you doing?" He would answer me, so I thought he was a nice guy. So one day I asked him if I could get a cigarette. "You want a cigarette? Yeah, no problem." They take away all your privileges. The next thing I know my cell gate is opening and he is there with another officer, and he goes, "Hey you want a cigarette?" So I looked at the other officer with him and I said to them, "Actually I quit smoking." He had a cigarette in his top pocket. "I brought you a cigarette here in my top pocket, I want you to come here and get it." I said, "Listen I quit smoking." He came inside. He had the other guard watch me and he started punching and kicking me on the floor. I was going with it; he really wasn't hurting me. I kept saying, "I'm sorry I'm sorry."

Anyway, I spent the whole 90-day sentence there. I lost track of the days. Now I am getting out and all I remember is one morning my cell is opening and the guard is saying "Get your things together you're outta here." No shoelaces, no belt, I had nothing. You walk down the corridor and they gave you your personal belongings my money, my watch, and stuff, and they said, "You're out!" At that time they had the ferry boat that took you to the other side. Now there's a bridge where they take you in a paddy wagon to drop you off. So when they dropped me off I needed to get home. I had some money and walked four or five blocks to a car service, and I said to the guy, "Drive me to New York." I asked for a cigarette from him and he gave it to me. I was whacked out of my brain; it was like smoking a joint.

When I was filming this documentary called "Hey Vinny" I had my friend Frank "Frankie the Butcher" Bonsangue in the boat with me. He said, "Where you taking me?" I said, "I want to show you where I went to college." He said, "Where'd you go?" I said, R.I. State" He said, "We're going to Rhode Island?" "What Rhode Island?" I said, " Nope, I'm talking about Rikers Island."

CHAPTER 11

THE MATZO BALL

So I couldn't fool around with the local Italian and Irish girls. I used to have to wait for the Jewish girls to come in from Forest Hills on the weekends. They used to hang out on McDougal Street. I said at least with them, they're not violent, so I won't end up in court. I at least got a chance to stay alive.

I would meet them, bring them over to sit on the stoop with them, kiss them, and smoke a joint. Nobody was around, it was a place to relax. It was pretty nice.

When I got out of Rikers I was like Don Cheech. They loved me back there at Tony Pastor's. They all said, "Hey that Vinny Vella is a stand-up guy."

I realized these guys didn't get arrested and I was the one getting arrested. Something is wrong with this conversation. How come they don't get arrested and I get arrested? I gotta be more slick or be a better actor. I actually started watching my Ps and Qs and being a little bit more slick about what I did.

I stopped robbing parking meters and cars and all this other stuff. I stopped taking envelopes.

I'm out of jail so I want to play a little bit.

The first Jewish girl I went out with lived in Forest Hills. I was dating her for a few months and after a while she says, "Vinny you got to do me a very big favor." I said, "Sure." She says, "My mother and father they want to meet you." I said, "That's no problem." "But I told them that you were Jewish." I said, "You told them I was Jewish; do they wear glasses?" "Please you've got to meet them. Could you say your name is something else other than Vinny Vella? Could you think of a Jewish name?" I said, "Yeah." So we had a lawyer at that time his name was Al Fisenhann, so my name was Al Fisenhann. She said, "You don't look like an Al Fisenhann." I shrugged my shoulders. So she told them my name was Al Fisenhann.

I caught the train and went out to Forest Hills and went to her apartment. Her father opened the door and looked at me from head to toe. I could tell what he was thinking. This fuckin' guy ain't Jewish. So after I walked in he said, "You don't look like an Al Fisenhann ." I said, "No, but I am."

So we sat down at the dining room table and her mother served a meal. We were eating and all of a sudden they come up with matzo ball soup. Never seen it, never heard of it, didn't know anything about it. So I see this thing, it was a big ball floating in the water. It was in a big bowl. Now I'm pushing it back and forth and my girlfriend is looking at me giving me motions like don't fuck around with that thing, cause I continued moving it around. So I'm looking around the table and they were all eating the soup, but not doing anything with the fucking ball. So I asked the father, "Do you eat this thing, or do you let it stay and float in the water?" He said, "Have you ever had matzo ball soup before?" I said, "Oh yeah." He says to me, "That's matzoh." I said, "You eat it?" He says, "What kind of a Jew are you?" I didn't know there were different kinds of Jews, so I said, "I'm the same kind of Jew that you are." He said, "That's matzo ball soup." I said, "Okay." I still didn't eat it. He started looking at his wife and looking over at his daughter.

Finally, he asked me to get up and he took me to the front door and he said, "Do me a favor, please. Take your Jewish religion someplace else and stay away from my daughter." I said, "No problem." As we were getting to the door, I heard the mother say to the daughter, "You stay away from him, you don't call him no more." I turned around and said, I'm religious." The mother says to me, "You're not Jewish, you wish you were Jewish, and don't come to this house no more. Leave my daughter alone."

I said to the father, "Before I leave could I ask you a question? Could you please tell me what was that thing in the wa-

Who's Better Than You!

ter?" He said, "Al or whatever your name is please leave. I don't need to answer these stupid questions," And he chased me out of the apartment.

I never got to find out about matzo ball soup and that big ball until I got to Miami Florida. That's when I met Rose and she was the one that educated me about the matzo ball and the soup.

CHAPTER 12

GREENWICH VILLAGE

Back in the 1960's you know I was into different types of music back then. I was into Motown, I was into some Bob Dylan music, Frank Sinatra, and Dean Martin songs. There was such a variety of music back then, life was so easy, and it was so beautiful back then. You had the Shirelles and Smokey Robinson and the Miracles. You had the Marvelettes and Diana Ross's Supremes.

Music and people were so beautiful back then and everything got screwed up when the Beatles came in and when companies started coming out with computers and all that shit. It ended up turning this world into a shithole.

To get into the Café Wha? back then it was like two dollars to get in and you'd sit down and be entertained. Richard Pryor would walk around, and the audience would put money in his hat for tips. Woody Allen was there. There was a place called Café Bizarre with all of the hippie music in there. You would find Richie Havens, the Mamas and Papas, and Peter Paul and Mary in there...

On McDougal Street at that time, there was all the cafés, cappuccino places, candy stores, and pizzerias. I hung out at a place called Rienzi's. It was one of my favorite places. It is no longer there. It was right across this street between Bleecker Street and Minetta Lane., across from the Kettle of Fish. I used to see Richard Pryor, The Monkees, Bill Cosby, Richie Havens, Woody Allen, Bob Dylan, and many more inside the Kettle of Fish. The Kettle of Fish moved to Third Street and finally to Christopher Street and that's where it is today. At Rienzi's for a dollar, you could hang out there all night. You'd hear music with people playing guitars. West 3rd Street was where all the nightclubs were. You had the: Heat Wave; the Purple Onion; the Goldbug, Cinderella; and Tony Pastor's which was a nightclub that also was a social club.

It was just so different, it was clean, it was nice, you can walk around the neighborhood carrying a $100 bill in your pocket and nobody would bother you back then. Everything changed rapidly like the rug was pulled out from under.

One day I saw this really attractive girl. At first, I thought it was a girl. Someone told me Vinny she's got one bigger than you have. I looked into her eyes.

Luckily, I didn't do anything.

CHAPTER 13

THE CARD GAME

So some of us went out to New Jersey to play in a card game. We didn't know all the guys but someone vouched for them. That is where I won my first car. I won a 51 Hudson Hornet. It looked like a hearse car. It was huge!

So during the game, the stakes got pretty high, so this guy put his title up for the Hudson. At that time I was about 14 years old. We were playing Acey-Deucey. That card game was also known as Between The Sheets or Maverick. You got two cards and you had to bet that when the next card was turned up, it would fall in between the first two.

So I won the car. The car was parked a couple of blocks away. After everybody left I got in the car and went to start it. There was no noise at all, nothing. We lifted up the hood and saw there was no battery. So I had to borrow another battery off of another car, in another block, come back, and put it in.

We were driving that car around the whole of Greenwich Village for the longest time. It got us all over and allowed us to get a lot of things done, but that's another story.

I had to get rid of that car cause that thing was a hog. It was huge, it was big, it was very noticeable. When that thing came down the street people looked at it and noticed that car. It was an old car, sort of banged up a little bit. It was dark gray.

After a while, I had to let go of that car because everything started going wrong with it. I brought it to this mechanic guy. He said it would cost me $60 for the repairs. Back then $60 was big money.

Meanwhile, the guy that gave me the pink slip for it during the game, his name was like "Tony" and the pink slip said "Eddie." It was a stolen car. I had no idea where this car came from. This is what the world was about back then. I says, "Hey mechanic, you wanna buy the car, I'll sell it to you." So of course he asked me for the title which caused a little confusion.

Shall we say, I sold the car at a discount.

CHAPTER 14

MY FRIEND ENZO "HOW TO SUCCEED"

My friend Enzo was dating this girl that was in this play called, *How to Succeed in Business Without Really Trying* on Broadway and 46th Street. He was 15, she was like 19 and she had a car. Now Enzo always lied to her and said he was 18. He had three phony licenses that showed he was 21, 29 and 38. He didn't even look like he was 15 years old. So he had this girl convinced that he had a license. When she asked, "Do you have a license?" He said, "Yeah I got a license." He always put his hand in his back pocket and never pulled out the license. So the girl said, "Could you do me a big favor? I have to go to work, so would you drive me to work at the theatre, then take the car, and then come pick me up later on." Enzo said, "Oh yeah!"

We were driving around in this car; it was like a Studebaker or something. All I remember was, that it was a shift, it wasn't a standard, there was drive and neutral. It was a stick in the front of the car. Back then they called them hydramatics.

We go back to pick her up after the play and we would have her wait, running late and all that other shit. He would convince her by saying, "Let me drive you home. I need the car, I got to go do a few things later and then I'll come pick you up in the morning and bring you back to work."

We had a grand time. We drove girls in the car, getting laid in the back seat. Oh man, what we didn't do with that car!

The relationship with her did not last very long. The girl was no longer in the play, and she had to move back to wherever she came from, and she had to take the car. So Enzo says, "Can I buy the car off of you?" She says, "Well…" He wanted to buy the car, so he used a couple of lines. He says, "Whatever you want, I'll pay you whatever money you want." and "Why don't you buy a new car 'cause this one is old." She goes, "Well I guess so." "How much do you want for the car?" She named her price. He says to her, "Can I pay you tomorrow? She trusted him so she said, "Sure".

The next day Enzo came back. I said to him, "How are you going to pay her today? He said, "Don't worry I am going to pay her today." I'm saying to myself where the freak did he get the money from? He has a check and I'm looking at the check but it had a different name on it. He hands the girl the check. The girl says, "Whose check is this?" Enzo said, "Oh,

My Friend Enzo "How to Succeed"

that's my uncle." He said this with a straight face. "My uncle gave me a check and said write it out to you." Oh God, I looking at him with a straight face thinking, oh man you're going to get this girl busted with this fucking check.

What he didn't do to this poor girl.

I always had to keep a straight face.

He ended up giving her the check and I thought wow Enzo is once again pulling another one on her. He was real slick.

Who's Better Than You!

CHAPTER 15

ON THE RUN TO FLORIDA

So the last thing I did when I was going on 18 years old, I beat these guys from Jersey. I sold them four pounds of catnip which looked just like marijuana. I put the marijuana on the top, so as soon as you ripped the packages open there was the marijuana. I put a layer of about five dollars of real pot on top of each pound. At that time marijuana was only $400 a pound. So I beat these guys for $1600. Me and Enzo, we sold them four pounds of catnip.

When we got the money we had to run real fast 'cause we knew when they would bring it back home to New Jersey and realize it's catnip, they're gonna come back looking for us. So Enzo and I run to the airport, and then we got to decide where we are going to go. So I said, "Let's go someplace where it's warmer." So we decided on Florida.

I'm still living home at the time, so I called my father when we landed, not my mother. She was always happy when I was out and away from the house. I always used to call him up at his store. I said, "Pop I'm okay, I'm down in Florida blah, blah, blah." So then I called my friend in the city and he said, "Vinny, there are some guys looking for you from Jersey." "Don't tell them where I am. Tell them I'm in California."

We were down there in Florida in Miami Beach. When I went down there at that time Miami Beach was all Jews and we were staying at a place down there called The Castaways at 116th St. and Collins Avenue. So we would take a bus all the way down to downtown Miami, down around Ocean Drive. Back then it was all the hotels facing the water and all the Jews sitting there in rocking chairs and they would criticize everybody that would walk by, and I was the only Gentile.

I decided it would be best to move to a downtown hotel. I was with my friend Enzo, and he didn't want to move downtown into the hotel. He knew this guy named Harvey a Jewish guy that we knew from New York who had moved down to Miami. My friend Enzo and Harvey start hanging out and he started getting high, not on pot, but on something else. That was when we started staying away from each other.

I checked into one of the hotels over there and it was only $25 a week. All you got in your room was a bed, a little fan, and a little black-and-white television. So one night I came out of the motel room and see all these Jews in rocking chairs. I walked by this little old Jewish lady, and I said, "Hello sweetheart. How are you doing?" "Oh, you called me sweetheart. You're a nice boy. Sit here, what's your name?" So I told her, and she says," "You're Jewish?" I said, "No I'm Italian, but I live in a Jewish neighborhood in New York."

They would criticize everybody that would walk by. If a girl walked by, they would say, "Look at how she is dressed. If my husband were alive and that was our daughter he'd break her legs." Back then they used to call these people "yentas" because they would blah, blah, blah, blah, and they would criticize you and everyone else. In Italian they would call them "chiacchierone."

I was the only Gentile there and they used to love me! They used to bring me down to Wolfie's 21, at 21st and Collins Avenue. They turned me on to pastrami, corned beef, brisket and all that Jewish food. They said come near the pool tomorrow. They would make things and sit by the pool with their hair up and they would chitchat. I used to hang out with them in the back near the pool. This one woman wanted me for herself. "Stay with me don't stay with them. They're no good." Her name was Rose, a little old Jewish woman. A beautiful woman. So we remained friends.

Then I got a job because I had to survive, my money was running out, and that $1600 could only last so long. I used to go into restaurants and steal tips off the tables.

Who's Better Than You!

So finally I got a job as a busboy at some Italian restaurant down there. Then the next thing you know I found this apartment on Normandy Isle, around 79th St. off Collins Avenue, and that Jewish woman Rose did not want me to leave the hotel. She said, "Stay here, I will pay your rent." She wanted me to stay with her. I told her that I would come back and visit her once a week. She always wanted to take me to the Jewish deli. There was another place there called Pumpernick's which was on Collins Avenue, and she'd take me there and turn me on to all this Jewish food. The first time she gave me matzo ball soup I still didn't know what it was. I looked at this ball floating in the water and I said, "Do you eat that or just leave it in the water?" So this other woman said, "What kind of a Jew are you?" I said, "I don't know. I don't know what to do with it." Rose said, "Don't tell her nothing." So the matzo ball mystery was finally solved by Rose. Most of the things I liked, some of the things I didn't.

So finally I moved back to New York 'cause I was running out of money. I still kept in touch with Rose. I used to call her up. One day I found out that she passed away and I immediately went back to Florida. They didn't have funerals like we had. They had a closed casket, and I was the only Gentile there again. I just felt so bad.

Then I wind up staying down there in Florida and get a

On the Run to Florida

job at a place called Moma Vivi's. At first, I was a busboy and then I was a kitchen helper doing preparation work with heads of lettuce and making dough.

Next thing you know I became a pizza man and started working in the restaurant.

Who's Better Than You!

CHAPTER 16

I'M ON VACATION FROM A VACATION

I was down in Miami Beach. My friend started fucking around with drugs and I was running out of money. I got a job down there and I'll never forget it. I met this guy, and he was at the Fontainebleau Hotel at that time in a bar there called the Poodle Lounge. I didn't know who he was or what he did there. I was a busboy and all that, and he kept telling me what to do. One day I said to him, "Why don't you fuck off, you Jew cocksucker! So I left that place right after that.

I seen Frank Sinatra before I finished my time at the Fontainebleau. I was hanging around, and I'll never forget it. I was at the hotel desk and the bellhop turned around and said, "Hey look there's Frank Sinatra." Then the bellhop ran up to him and said, "Hey Frank." Then Frank broke away from the bodyguard and he hit the guy right in the mouth, knocked him down, and was kicking and punching him. He said, "You called me Frank, you motherfucker! You call me Mr. Sinatra!" I thought oh fuck,

Who's Better Than You!

I didn't want to go up and say nothing to him.

Now the next thing you know I was down with all the Jews in Miami Beach.

I run across this one guy, he was Italian, and his name was Bobby. He said, "Are you Italian?" I said, "Yeah." What are you doing down here?" "I'm on vacation." "Where do you come from?" "From New York." "What kind of work do you do?" "Right now I'm not working." "What are you on vacation from a vacation? Did you do something back there? Is anybody looking for you?" I said, "I'm not too sure." He said, "You plan on staying down here?" I said, "Yeah." He goes, "Are you looking for a job?" I said, "Yeah that would be good." He said, "Meet me tonight at a place called the Wreck Bar it's up on 163rd St. and Collins Avenue."

There were all Italians in there. Bobby said, "I'm gonna make you a maître d'." I didn't even know what a maître d' was. When he told me maître d' I thought I had to wear a skirt. I didn't know what the hell it was. It was at the Castaways Hotel. This was in the 1960s. He says, "I'll teach you how to be a maître d'. I said, "Bobby I don't know what a fucking maître d' is." He said, "You come here in the afternoon you answer phones, we got 20 tables in here, you get the people's names, you assign them to a table. I'm going to tell you how to get a tip. At night always keep like five or six good tables for your-

I'm On a Vacation From a Vacation

self and if a guy comes in and he says, "Hi, I'd like a table." You say, did you make a reservation? If the guy says, "No." Then you put your hand in your pocket and you're going to make a tip. If he don't get what you're doing, give him a table wherever you want to." I said, "Okay."

So when I became the maître d' some guy comes in and says, "I need a table and I said, "Do you have a reservation?" He goes "No." I say, "Well then I don't know if I can help you out." "You can't help me out?" The guy sees me put my hand in my pocket, takes the hint and says, "Maybe this will take care of it." He gives me a tip and I say, "Oh I'll get a table for you right away." So I got him a nice table and I got a nice tip.

That same night that I started the plan was for me to meet the owner for the first time. His name was Harvey M. So Bobby said "You're going to meet the owner tonight." I said, "All right fine." I go in the office I see that they're all Italian except for Harvey M. who is sitting behind the counter. He's the one I called a Jew cocksucker, motherfucker, fuckin' Jew at the Fontainebleau. When I saw him I went like this OHHHHH! NOOOOO! So Bobby says to me, "I want to introduce you." So the guy says, "Oh no, we met before." I said, "I'm sorry." So they were talking for a while, him and the Italian guys and one says to me, "You called him Jew motherfucker?" I said, "I didn't know who he was." He said, "Listen to me, you don't call nobody no Jew motherfucker! If you ever call him or anyone else a Jew motherfucker around here you know what we'll do to you? We gonna take off your fucking clothes and we're gonna throw you in the swamp with the alligators. This way they don't spit up your fucking shoes and belt so you can't be identified. You have a lot of respect for this guy, you hear? Apologize!" I said, "I'm sorry."

So Harvey M. says, "I heard they're going to make you into the maître d'. Now I want to have a talk with you." So I thought they're going to smack the shit out of me. So he takes me outside and there were these wooden beams. He says, "You see that wooden beam up there?" I said "Yeah." He said, "Do you see what's up there?" There were three little jars up there. He says, "Two of them are empty, but the first one, you know what's in there?" I said "What?" He said, "A finger." I said, "A finger?" He says, "Yeah we caught a guy stealing so when we caught him stealing, we pickled his finger. Now he doesn't work here no more." So he says, "Now the next jar is going to have two fingers in it, so if you want to work here I would expect you not to steal. If you decide you don't want to work here, you leave here now, we're friends and I've got a lot of respect for you, but if you decide you wanna work here, I'll expect you not to steal. You want the job, or you don't want the job?" "Yeah," I said, "I want the job." He said, "Re-

I'm On a Vacation From a Vacation

member don't steal!" He said, "There is this one other thing too, "If you ever find any money on the floor don't ever think it's yours. This is my place you pick it up, don't put it in your pocket, you hold it up in the air and you go over to the bar and you tell the bartender to give you an empty envelope, you put it in the envelope behind the bar and when I come in at night you tell me about it." I said, "Okay fine."

So I wind up working there.

It was about three weeks later. I see there was a $10 bill on the floor. I picked the fucking thing up and I carried it over to the bar. So when Howard came in I said, "Howard I found $10." He said, "Where?" "Over there." He said, "What did you do?" "I picked it up like you told me, I held it up in the air went over to the bar, and I put it in an envelope." When we got over to the bar he opened up the envelope and took the $10 bill out. He put the bill in his jacket. Then he went in his pocket and he gave me three dollars. I said, "What's that for?" He said, "That's for finding the $10. I said, "I get three dollars?" He said, "What are you my fucking partner?" He said, "You found the money in my place. You didn't find it in your place. You found the money in my fucking joint." I took the three dollars and I said, "Thank you so much."

So one day it was about four o'clock in the afternoon, there was no one in there and some fucking cops come in. One cop said, "What's your name?" I said, "Vinny Vella." "What are you doing here?" I said, "I came in here looking for a job." "Listen don't lie to us, we came in here a few times, and you were here." I said, "That's because the owner was never here so I keep coming back." They said, "Do yourself a favor and get whatever belongs to you and get the fuck out of here. Don't come back in here again."

They closed the place down that night. They closed it for a few days. All of a sudden I get a call from Bobby and he goes "Did you say anything?" I said, "No I didn't say nothing. I didn't say a fucking word man." He said, "What did you tell em?" I said, "I was looking for a job and you know the owner never shows up around here." So Bobby says, "We're gonna open up tomorrow at three o'clock."

I said to myself I don't want to get pinched here. I already got my friend saying to me that they're looking for me in New York. I can't go back home.

I'm thinking that I'm going to hell no matter where I go.

CHAPTER 17

MR. SINATRA

Then I started at a place called Jilly's. This was back in 1966. I went from the frying pan into the oven.

Jilly's was owned by Frank Sinatra's best friend. So I started working over there. It was on Treasure Island. When I applied for the job I said I was working at the Wreck Bar at the Castaways. The hiring guy said, "Wait a second are you Vinny Vella from New York?" "Yeah," I said. He said, "Wait a second. You know we heard about you. You got a tight mouth don't you." "Whaddya mean a tight mouth?" "The cops came in there. What did ya tell them?" "I told them I'm going for a job." He says, "Whaddya looking for here?" I said, "I'd like to break in here as a maître d'." He says, "We already got a maître d'. Let me take your name if anything, I'll call ya." True enough three days later he called and said, "Tell me about the maître d' thing with the hand in the pocket." I told him and I got the job.

So one night this guy comes in and says, "Do you have a

table?" I said, "Did you make a reservation?" He says, "No it's for Frank." I said, "It don't matter who it's for." I didn't know who he meant when he said Frank. I said, "Frank? Well, I'm sorry I don't have anything for ya." He said, "Did you hear what I said?" "I heard you; you says Frank." "He said, "Listen to me, you get me a table, or I'll get you fired!" "What do you mean fired? How are you going to get me fired? If you don't make reservations you can't have…" He cut me off and said, "Listen to me it's for Frank, Frank Sinatra, he's Jilly's best friend!" I said, "Please, forgive me sir, you only said Frank, I didn't hear Sinatra. Okay, I'll have a table for you right away. That's you right there in the front." He said, "I don't want that table, I want the other table!" I said, "There's people sittin' on it." He said, "Tell the people you made a mistake and push them over." I said to myself, oh fuck here we go 'cause everyone in the place looked like wise guys to begin with. I knew I was up shit's creek when I started. So I went over to the table and said, "The guy who gave you that table made a mistake." They said to me, "That was you, you put us here!" So I said, "Sorry I made a mistake, move over there, and we'll give you an extra drink." They moved over.

So meanwhile the guy goes outside and brings in Frank Sinatra, with two guys around him. Frank wasn't a very big guy, and he says, "Is this the guy?" I figured he's going to

Mr. Sinatra

smack me. He said, "What's your name?" I said, "Vinny." He gave me a $100 bill. They all went and sat down. He was drinking Jack Daniels. About a half hour later the guy comes up to me and says, "Frank wants you to come over and join him for a drink at the table." So I said, "I can't sit down." He said, "You sit down, don't worry about it." I say, "If the boss comes in, I'm gonna get fired." "Well you ain't gonna get fired, sit down!" he said.

So then Jilly walks in. I'm trying to get up and this guy's holding me down and Jilly's gesturing to me to get up. I said," Jilly I'm sorry, they asked me to stay here." He said, "Don't worry about it." When he walked in as I said, Frank gave me a $100 tip. Oh, man! I didn't even make that much money in a week! With the tips, I made like $75 a week. He gave me a hundred dollars! So I figured the least I could do for him is buy him the bottle of wine that he already had at his table. That was about 45 or 50 bucks out of the hundred. I told Jilly when he came in," I'll pay for it." Jilly, he says, "Don't worry about it, he doesn't pay for anything, keep it, don't worry about it." So I kept the hundred. And as he was walking out Frank goes "Hey Benny." I said, "It's Vinny." He said, "Here's another hundred, save your money. So altogether he gave me a total of $200. I thought, oh fuck maybe I should follow him out to the parking lot and everything else.

Who's Better Than You!

You know when he first came into the Wreck Bar I was like wow. He's like really Frank Sinatra and when he gave me $100 tip that was like when Frank Sinatra became everything to me. Back then I had two types of music. Frank Sinatra, Dean Martin, Tony Bennett and Motown. Motown was my favorite. I was into Marvin Gaye, the Supremes, the Shirelles, the Marvelettes. I was into all of that shit. Gary U.S. Bonds was on my Manhattan Cable TV Show too.

Several years went by and I'm going to see Sinatra at Carnegie Hall. I bought some $18 tickets in the bloody nose section up in the balcony. So I'm there with this girl waiting to go in and all of a sudden she says, "Isn't that Frank Sinatra?" We walked down the street a little bit and he's coming out of a limo and I ran right up to him. He looks at me and he goes, "Hey what are you doing here? Didn't I see you down in Florida?" I said, "Yeah I live here in New York." "What's your name, oh yeah it's Benny." I said to myself I should change my name to Benny. "My name is Vinny; you keep calling me Benny." He said, "What, are you correcting me?" I thought you can call me anything you want. You can call me Suzy for a $100 tip. I said, "No, matter of fact Benny that's my middle name, call me Benny, call me whatever you want." He said, "What are you doing here? I said, "Well, I got tickets to come and see you today." He says, "Where are the tickets?" So I

Mr. Sinatra

showed him the tickets. He must have realized they were way up in the balcony. So he took them and he ripped them up into a hundred pieces.

Somebody said, "Come on Frank it's time to go." I said to him, "Well that's my only way in." He said, "You go to the door, you tell them I sent you and they'll put you in the front." And then he walked away.

What do I do now? I walked to the door and thought, what am I going to tell them? So I went to the front door, and I tell the guy, "Frank Sinatra ripped up my tickets into a hundred pieces. He said to talk to someone at the front door." The guy said, "What's your name?" "I got a couple of names, I go by Benny and Vinny, Vinny, Benny. Frank Sinatra said for me to see you." So he let us in, and said, "Come with me." I followed him, and he put us in the front row seats. My date was definitely impressed. She said, "You know Frank Sinatra"? I didn't want to tell her the whole story, so I said, "Oh we're buddies from way back."

He never said hello to me, but he acknowledged me with his eyes when he was up there singing on the stage.

Who's Better Than You!

CHAPTER 18

MY FATHER

When he was younger my father used to race bicycles at the Velodrome at Madison Square Garden.

My father was a gem. My mother used to beat the shit out of me, but my father never once did he ever put his hands on me. I used to say, "Ma can I have money." She would yell, "Get the hell out of here. Go get a job you sonamabitch, instead of being like a bum all the time." My father used to say, "Go get the hell out of here, get a job" and then he used to pull out a 5 or 10-dollar bill and put the money in my hand. He was the best. When I went away to Otisville State Training School for Boys, Rikers Island, Mount Lorretta, it would always be my father that would come to see me.

My mother came to Rikers Island one time to see me. I told them to take her off the visiting list. I don't want her to come anymore. She came there one time and rather than say hello Vinny, how are you, how do you feel, is everything okay? No. She said, "I tell a you, you see this is where you belong, this is where you came, you learn your lesson, you don't do this, you don't do that, you never listen to me." "Look," I said, "Hey Ma, do me a favor. Hey, go home. And you know what, don't you come here no more. Don't worry about it."

In those days you weren't allowed phone calls. Today they got televisions in the cell. They didn't have those things in those days. No such things as telephones and all that shit. They didn't allow filtered cigarettes. Nothing! So my father comes and says, "What did you tell your mama." I said, "Yeah, she came here breaking my balls and I told her not to come no more."

My father used to work on an ice truck. They didn't have refrigerators back then, they had ice boxes. He worked for some ice company. Trucks used to come down the street and ring a bell, like a cowbell. People used to yell out the window, "Louie I need ice, I need ice." He chopped up a piece, put it in a burlap bag on his shoulder, then he'd go up four or five flights, and deliver ice. Then later on he made money. He was a penny pincher. Don't forget this was going on during the Depression. Then he bought a pushcart. Then he was selling his own ice. He rang his cowbell, "Louie I need ice." He took about four or five long pieces of ice, broke it, and chopped it. He used the pushcart to push his ice up and down the streets.

Then later on after he made more money he opened up a store, Louie's Fish Market at 131 Mott Street between Grand

My Father

and Hester Streets. He had the store for 41 years. When he opened the store his rent was like $37 a month. It was a fish market and he left it in the 70s. He used to work by himself in the fish market and then once in a while, I would have to help him. I would come in on a Friday and watch outside of the store. He had the clams and the mussels outside and he would work inside. He says. "You don't want to go to school sonamabitch, you gotta come work in the fish market." I used to work in the fish market on Friday and he used to give me $10 for the day. My sisters were married at that point. One sister had moved to Iselin, New Jersey, and the other sister had moved to the Bronx. Then there were my two brothers, one was in California and the other one was in Pennsylvania. After the day in the fish market was over, between tips and deliveries I'd make $15 or $20. That was good money back then.

Then I used to go to Broadway Central. It was like four or five dollars a night for a hotel room. I used to bring a girl. First I'd bring her out to eat, go to the bar order anything on the top shelf, go to a movie, then go to the hotel and still have two or three dollars left at the end of the night. This was during the 60's and I'd have some fuckin' money left.

Now when my father was ready to give up the fish market, there was this girl that I wanted to date for the longest time. Finally, I got a date with her. When you deal with fish, that shit gets underneath your nails and whatever. I finally got a date with her after all those years and I went out with her that night and I'm saying, "Oh thank God," and I pick her up and she says, "I don't feel good, I feel nauseous, I smell fish." I lost the date with her; she went home.

Now my father was getting ready to give up the fish market. He wanted to leave me the fish market. I turned it down. So he said he didn't want to sell it to the Chinese. There were all these Chinese buying out the other stores around it so he said, "I'm a not gonna sell it, whoever wanna buy the store they gotta be Italian." I said, "Pa, no Italian is going to buy the store, the fuckin' Chinese are around here." "They gotta be Italian or I'm a not gonna sell." So he stood there for a few more years surrounded by the Chinese. They were like givin the shit away. The Chinese had fish market after fish market. So he wanted $125,000 for the business. There was this one Chinese guy who kept coming in and he wanted to buy the store. "I'm a not gonna sell it to you, anyone whose gonna buy this store they gotta be Italian." My father was like an Archie Bunker. "If you wanna buy the store it'll cost you $250,000." The guy came back like two weeks later with $250,000, cash money. He had the money. The guy not only bought the store, he also bought the building too. At that time the buildings were $40,000 $50,000 and $60,000. Now the guy is trying

My Father

to buy any building around there. Today they are anywhere from $2 million on up. So my father sold out to the Chinese. He wanted to leave me the store and I said, "No, no, no, I appreciate it, Dad."

I had already learned about dating and working in a fish store.

Who's Better Than You!

CHAPTER 19

BELLEVUE PSYCHIATRIC HOSPITAL – LOCKED UP

Around 1970 I have my cousin Angelo on drugs. He flipped out on acid, speed, or whatever the fuck he had. When we realized that he was freaking out, I was married to my first wife. She was Jewish and at the time she was pregnant. He would call her up and say, "When I see you on the street I'll stick a knife in you, and I'll kill you and the baby." My wife would call me up and tell me what he said. I would follow up by calling him up and asking him if he had called her. He would say, "I didn't call her. "Are you crazy?" I said to my wife, "Honey are you sure it's him?" She said, "Honey I know his voice, that was him." So that went on about three or four times. I said, "All right you know what I'll do. I'll get a recorder. Every time that somebody rings the phone, before you answer push this button it will start the recording and when they finish talking you push stop. If it is somebody you know like a friend after you push start you don't have to record the conversation, just push stop."

So one day he says to her on the phone, "You can tell your husband whatever you want, but if I see you in the street I'll come up right behind you and stick this knife right in you. I'll kill you. You're a fucking slut," and you're this and you're that. Now after I listened to the recording I knew it was him. I told my aunt and uncle. I said, "He's cracking up, I got him on tape." I let them listen to it. My aunt said, "He's act a little strange over here too. What is he doing calling her up?"

Next thing you know he's got locked up for vagrancy three or four times. Then he got sent to Bellevue Psychiatric Hospital. My aunt calls me up, "Vinny please you do me a favor, they find Angelo, they lock him up again, they put him in a Bellevue. You go see him over there. Maybe if you go over there that might help out a bit. I can't go my legs they're a killing me, they hurt me, and your uncle just came home from work so he cannot go." I was living on St. Marks Place at that time. I said, "No, please I don't want to." She said, "C'mon Vinny please do me that big a favor." I said, "All right, all right."

So I went to go see that crazy bastard in the fuckin' hospital. I go in there. They gave me my pass. So I see he's in a lockup ward. My identification was in my jacket pocket and I went into his room and sat down. Everyone there they all had their individual rooms. I sit down for a while and Angelo says,

Bellevue Psychiatric Hospital - Locked Up

"Come on, I'll show you around the place." I said, "Let me get my jacket." He said, "Don't go for your jacket, nobody will come into the room, leave it there." I left everything in there, my jacket and all my identification, everything.

We walked into the day room. They're all sitting down watching TV, rocking back and forth, one of them directing traffic, one giving rules, some talking to themselves, and the others talking a whole bunch of shit. Angelo he says, "I got to go to the bathroom." He said to me as if I knew the answer. "Where is the bathroom?" I looked around and said, "Right over there." So, Angelo goes to the bathroom. I was definitely watching him to see what he was up to.

So, this guy comes over and he is sitting next to me and he said, "Are you visiting here too?" I said, "Yeah," He said, "Who are you visiting?" I said, "I'm visiting my cousin." "Yeah, I'm visiting my cousin too. How often do you come here?" "Well, this is the first time I came here." He said, "What's your name?" I said, "Vinny," I said, "What's your name?" He said, "I have a lot of names." I was like in this deep conversation with him and all of a sudden he says, "If you need anything here just let me know. I can help you out." Oh man, another fuckin nut. I said to him, "Get the fuck out of here." Then one of the nurses came by pointing her finger to her head motioning that he's cuckoo.

Who's Better Than You!

I waited for my cousin for five, maybe ten minutes. I'm looking for Angelo. Where the fuck is he? My cousin was supposed to be in the bathroom, but now he's gone. I'm looking now all over this fucking place and he's gone. So I went into the bathroom. No Angelo. Now I want to get the fuck out of here, so I go back to the room to get my jacket, and my jacket has gone missing with all my identification, my wallet, and the pass.

So, there was this guard that sat in front near the entrance door. The door was about 6 feet away and there was a yellow line. So when I went across the yellow line to talk to him, the guard said, "Stand behind the yellow line." I said, "No you don't seem to understand. I came here to see my cousin." He said, "Get behind the yellow line!" I said, "What is it with you and the yellow line! I came to visit my cousin and he took my fuckin' pass." And again he said to me, "Get behind the yellow line!" So I got behind the yellow line and I said, "Could you hear me?" I came here to visit my cousin, he took my fuckin' wallet, my pass, and everything. Now I am here with all these fuckin' maniacs. I got to get out of here, I got to get to work! "Why do I have to stand behind the yellow line for? I'm fucking talking to you!" I got to get the fuck out of here! I got to go to work." "Just stay behind the yellow line!" "What the fuck is it with you and this yellow line." So I went behind the yellow

Bellevue Psychiatric Hospital - Locked Up

line. I said, "Can you hear me from here!" I said, "I came to visit my cousin and his name is Angelo Vella and he took my jacket and all my identification. I'm here and you keep telling me to stand behind the yellow line. I got to get the fuck out of here!" The guard said, "Do yourself a favor, and do me a favor, go back to your room." "I don't have a fuckin' room!" And this went on for the longest time. Then there was this announcement. "Everybody go stand near your room." "I don't have a fuckin' room!" The guard says, "Go to your room!"

Then all of a sudden a bell rang off or something. They're giving out the medication and the staff are walking down the corridor with trays and all that. A woman came over and said, "Stand near your room." I was standing in the middle between rooms. I said, "I don't have a room. "I don't know why I have to stand there when they're giving out medication." I said, "I ain't taking no fucking medication! Who is that medication for?" She said, "Angelo Vella it's for you." "You know what, all you people are fucking crazy. I came here to visit my cousin, he took my jacket, he took everything, and he left and I'm going to become that Angelo Vella. I am Vinny Vella!" I lifted up my sleeve to show them I had a tattoo with my name Vinny. The aide said, "That could be your father's name." So I said, "You know there is something wrong with you. Listen to me, I came in to visit that sick bastard. He took my fuckin' pass; this one over here is telling me to get behind the fuckin' yellow line. I got to get out of here. I am not Angelo! You know there is something fucking wrong with you." So now a woman is handing out medication. And she says, "If you don't stand by your room you'll be sedated." I said, "Don't give me that medication. It's Friday and I'm gonna become Angelo Vella by the time Monday comes. That prick is gonna be outside and be Vinny Vella and I'm gonna become the fucking nut directing traffic and everything else in here."

So as they continued handing out the medication I said to the nurse, "Sweetheart please, I don't want to give you a hard time, but the guy at the door's telling me to get behind the yellow line. I'm trying to tell him I'm not Angelo Vella. Do you know Angelo Vella? She said, "No, who's Angelo Vella?" "He's the one that had this room, and this guy told me to go stand by my room because you're handing out medication. I am not Angelo Vella. I am Vinny Vella!" I pushed up my sleeve "You see it says, Vinny. He stole my pass and all my identification, and he left, and I'm stuck here. And now I'm not going to take no medication." "Well, there could be a problem then." I said, "Listen to me, there's got to be somebody here who knows Angelo Vella?"

This is on a Friday and I'm fucked between doctors, nurses, medication and the guy at the front door. "Please do not have me take this medicine. I'll be so fucked up I won't be able to talk my way out of here no more." The nurse said, "I'll hold the medication till the last one and I'll try to find out if anybody knows Angelo Vella."

Somebody else in the meantime comes over to me and says, "Who are you?" I said, "My name is Vincent Vella. I came here to visit my cousin and that dumb fucking crazy bastard took my pass, took all my identification walked out of here and I can't leave. He left me with all these morons here. That guy over there keeps telling me to stand behind the yellow line, this one's looking to give me medication. I want to get out of here, I got to go to work. My aunt told me to come to see my cousin. Why don't you call her up and ask her who came to visit." He says, "Well, you know…" I'm showing him the tattoo and he says, "That really doesn't mean too much." I said, "Do you know my cousin?" He said, "Nope." "I said do you take pictures of these morons when they come in? That one wants to give me medicine, that one wants me to get behind the yellow line. I gotta get out of here! Listen, how about does he have a doctor or anybody that fucking knows him? I ain't taking no medication, I don't want to be sedated. Listen to me. Do I look fuckin' crazy to you?" This guy says, "Yeah."

He then says, "Oh let me see what I can do, wait here."

"Wait here? I can't go fuckin' anywhere!" "Wait here!"

Who's Better Than You!

Meanwhile, an administrator comes over to me and says, "Who are you?" I said, "I already went through this whole thing." I had to go through it again. I said, "My name is Vincent Vella, I came in to visit a sick fuckin' member of my family, he's crazy, his name is Angelo Vella. I left my identification, and my wallet, everything in his room, he went to the bathroom came back took my identification and everything and he left and I'm stuck in here. This one wants to give me medication and they're telling me I'm going to be sedated. This guy is telling me to stand back behind the yellow line. I got to get out of here! I got to go to work!"

"Wait, I know somebody that knows him. Just wait." "I can't get the fuck out of here. How long do I gotta wait? You're the third person already, I don't want to stay in here for the weekend."

Now they are ringing bells, people are going to eat, and guys are flipping hard-boiled eggs in the hallway. Get the fuck out of here! I gotta get the fuck outta here.

A guy comes out and he says, "Who are you? I said, "I'm Vincent Vella, I have a cousin here, Angelo Vella." "Oh, Angelo is your cousin?" I said, "You know him?" "Yeah, I know him. You know he told me you were coming." "I came here to visit; he took my jacket and he walked out of here. That guy's telling me to stand behind the yellow line. They're all telling me I'm going to be sedated. This one wants to give me medicine, The other ones are telling me to wait. I keep talking to this one, that one. I gotta get out of here!"

He says, "All right I'll put an end to this right away." He says, "Let me go and see what I can do. Wait here". "Where the fuck do you think I'm gonna go? I can't go nowhere! What do you mean you're going to go? Please don't go home now, it's Friday and I won't see you till Monday. I don't want to be here for the weekend." He says, "Don't worry I'll be back."

He leaves and about a half-hour to forty minutes later he came back with another administrator. I said, "Do you know Angelo Vella?" She said, "Sure I know him." "Well, I am Vinny Vella and I have to get out of here." I repeated the whole thing and said, "Do I look nuts?"

Before I left I said to the administrator, "You can take the medication, you know what, give it to that guy near the door." Then I looked at him and I said, "You see I told you I wasn't fuckin' crazy. You and your fucking yellow line!"

They finally let me out.

So I went home and my aunt says to me, "Angelo, Come sta?" (Angelo, how is he?) "How is he?" I said, "That little motherfucker had me locked up in the nut house." She said, "How is he doing?" "He's doing okay. I was in there for four hours. He had me locked up. He took my jacket, my wallet, identification and everything. He walked out."

I had to get all new identification and that nut was out in the streets with my identification.

CHAPTER 20

NEW ORLEANS LOCK UP

About a month or two months later after the Bellevue lock up Aunt Concetta said, "Vinny do me a big a favor." "What. Angelo again? Now what?" "They find Angelo. They find him in New Orleans. He's a walkin' the streets. There not gonna let him out unless somebody go and pick him up." "Aunt Concetta, no please I ain't going to fuckin' New Orleans. I don't even know where the fuckin' New Orleans is." "Whatever you do, you got to go get him. I pay for the airfare. I pay whatever you got to do. Please go get him." I said, "I don't know where the New Orleans is!" Aunt Concetta said, "His father, he can't go 'cause he gotta work."

So I said, "Leave me the number of the police station." I called them up and they said they picked him up for vagrancy. "The only way they're gonna let him out is if someone comes and gets him," I told my aunt. She goes, "Vinny please I pay the airfare; I pay everything. Please you go get him, bring him home please." I said, Aunt Concetta pleeeeze!"

I went home that night and my wife says to me, "Where are you going now? I said, "They locked him up again. I got to go to New Orleans." She says, "Don't take your fuckin' identification, don't go near him, don't do this, don't do that."

I flew to New Orleans. I went against my principles. I could see myself behind bars. I really didn't want to go. Like a jerk, I went to the jail. Inside, all these nut jobs are walking past me down the corridor. Behind the glass, they're all looking at me walking by and waving to me. Meanwhile, like a jerk, I'm waving to all of them. It looked like maybe I knew them or something. I had no idea.

So finally when I get to the guy in charge and ask about my cousin, the cop says, "He has two identifications, Angelo Shotwell and Angelo Vella." I said, "Listen, he's Angelo Vella, he's fucked up here in the head, he is not Angelo Shotwell." So we go and sit in a room. Angelo comes out with a straight face and the cop says to him, "Your cousin is here to pick you up." Angelo at the time is totally bald on top, has a beard, blond hair on the side, and green eyes, so he looked nothing like me. So he says, "Who is my cousin?" The cop points at me and Angelo says, "He's not my cousin. He looks nothing like me." The cop said, "He says he's not your cousin, besides he doesn't look anything like you." I said, "Listen to me. You think I got nothing else better to do besides come from

New Orleans Lock Up

New York to pick up a fuckin' nut job. Unfortunately, he's my cousin. He's crazy!" The cop says, "I don't know what to do. I don't know what to tell you." So Angelo refuses to come with me. I said, "Let me talk to him for two minutes by myself and I will prove he's not Angelo Shotwell. Believe you me I will get him to admit who he is." The officer says, "Don't put your hands on him." I say, "I'm not gonna touch him."

I took Angelo to the side, and I said, "Let me tell you something you sick motherfucker. You want to be Angelo Shotwell? You can be Angelo Shotwell and they're going to keep you in this fuckin' place until you're sane, and all your marbles come back. That will take a long time because you're fucked up. Then they'll let you out. If you are Angelo Vella I can take you out today. Now if you want to be Angelo Shotwell and tell them I'm not your cousin, that's fine. I'll go back to New York. You know what? You can go fuck yourself with all these other fucking morons or you can tell them you're Angelo Vella and come home with me. Now what are you gonna tell them? Which is it gonna be because I don't give a fuck. I'm gonna go home and you'll stay here." He went over to the officer and said, "Yeah he's my cousin."

They brought him to the airport with handcuffs and put him on the plane. Meanwhile, he's all dirty. As soon as the plane landed in New York, he took off. I said "Where are you going? He said, "Downtown." "Your mom told me to bring you home." He said, "I'll be home later" and he took off on me.

I got home and my aunt starts with, "Dov'è Angelo? (Where's Angelo?) "He told me he was Angelo Shotwell and when he got off the plane he said he would be home later." "How's he look". "Same way he always looked; except he had a beard." 'Why'd he have a beard?" "How the fuck do I know. He didn't shave. That's why he had a beard. He was dirty." "Where did he go?" "I don't know. I don't know where he is. I got him out." My aunt says, "Do me a favor." "Stop with the do me a favor. When he gets locked up don't call me. Let him stay there for a while. Let them give him medication so he straightens out a little bit."

He's been wacky ever since up to today. I was over his house one day and I wasn't feeling well, and he said, "You want some aspirin? I said, "I don't want nothing from here."

My uncle before he died, he said to me, "Vinny please do me a favor, you know nobody likes Angelo, nobody a talk to him because of the way he is, please do me a favor if anything should happen to me please keep an eye on him, make sure nobody hurt him, make sure he's okay. I said, "You can guarantee that you can rest in peace, God forbid if anything happens I'll look out after him. You're the best father to him, you did a great job. You're the best father that anybody could want."

New Orleans Lock Up

When Angelo does something messed up today, I look at the picture of my uncle and I say, "I'm doing you a favor and if it wasn't for you, I'd kill him."

So I do it for my uncle.

Who's Better Than You!

CHAPTER 21

MOM AND THE EIGHT MILLION DOLLAR LOTTERY TICKET

Back in the '70s, my mother would always buy the lottery tickets. She always used to give me the tickets. I used to get the numbers from the lottery place, and I would bring them home and check them with her numbers.

I don't know what ever made me do it differently this way, one day. I always did it the same way. I got the numbers from the lottery place and checked them with her. But this one time she had the tickets from the previous drawing, and I wrote down those numbers on an envelope she had lying around. So I went to the lottery place on Sunday morning. I pulled out the envelope and was writing down all kinds of numbers, the Pick Three, the Pick Five, The Pick Four, all these other numbers. Her numbers were there too. And I forgot I wrote them all down from the previous drawing.

So now when I went back to the house and I'm thinking

that I wrote those numbers down there at the lottery place. I didn't think I wrote them down at her house because I always did it the same way. So when I got upstairs she said to me in Italian," Hai controllato i numeri?"(Did you check the numbers?). I said, "Oh yeah." So I pulled the ticket out, you know the envelope that had all the numbers on it, and I am looking at it not realizing that those were her numbers that I wrote 'em down to play for her, and I'm thinking that I wrote them down from the lottery place. So I am checking them, and I say, "Hey Ma, ya got one number here, you got two, you got, wait, you got three numbers, Ma ya got four numbers, Ma you got five numbers, Ma you ain't gonna believe you got all the numbers!" She was hollering in Italian. The prize was like EIGHT MILLION DOLLARS!

She freaked. She called her sister in Italy, my brother Louie in California, my sister in Boston, and my other brother in Pennsylvania. She called everybody. I said to her, "Put this ticket in a safe place, I'll come and get you tomorrow morning. In Italian she said, "Non preoccuparti, lo metterò proprio qui" (Don't worry I gonna put it right here.) "Non preoccuparti. (Don't worry.) Nobody's gonna find it! I put it in a safe place." At that time I was a milkman and she said, "Quit a your job. I don't want you driving the goddam truck, you're gonna get killed. Quit a your job!"

Mom and the Eight Million Dollar Lottery Ticket

So that same day I quit my job. I called this guy named John and I said, "John you know what you can do with that sour milk and that buttermilk and that sour cream. Stick it up your wife's ass!" I just gave it to him.

So the next morning I stopped at the lottery place to get some more scratch-offs or whatever. I'm looking at the numbers that came out and she had some very simple numbers like 2, 3, 9, 15, 25 and I'm looking at the numbers and it said 30, 33, 40, 47, 51. I'm looking at the numbers posted on the wall and I say to the guy, "When did those numbers come out?" He said, "Those were the numbers that came out Saturday night." I said, "It can't be, my mother won. Those weren't the numbers, she had like 3,9,15." He says, "Where did you play?" "I played the New York lottery," I said. He said, "Those are the numbers that came in." I said, "Give me a printout." He gave me a printout. That's when I turned over the envelope where I had all those numbers on it. I turned it over because my mother every time she got mail she would take the back of the envelope and open it up and use it for scrap paper near the phone. I realize now that it was on one of her pieces of scrap paper. When I turned it over and saw my last name on the back Vella, V-E-L-L-A. Now it hit me, now I'm realizing, Oh Shit!, I'm in a lot of fuckin' trouble. I wrote those numbers down over here on this envelope.

Who's Better Than You!

So when I went to see her on Monday her hair was all teased, and she was ready to go out the door to claim her prize of EIGHT MILLION DOLLARS!

I said, "Ma I have to tell you something." "Whaddya gone a tell me. Come on let's go I got a lotta things to do today." Ma there is a terrible mistake." "What a mistake?" I said you didn't win." "What you think you're gonna fuck a me for eight million dollars! Oh please, she used language like you would never believe. "Ma," I said, "Nobody's trying to do anything to ya, I made a terrible mistake. You did not win." "You come out over here, you don't come to someplace else. I know you too good." I said, "Ma these aren't the numbers. She says, "LOUIE!" She called my father and said," Run downstairs and go get a the numbers." She called me every name in the book. I don't even know if I should even repeat what she said. She said, "You cock a sucker, you no come in this house no more." I said, "Ma would you stop cursing I made a mistake." "You fuck up in the head, that's your problem!"

She screamed at me, "I called my sister in Italy, I called my brother, I called Louie in California. You're a no come into this house no more until you pay the phone bill: because you a sonamabitch. Where you get a these numbers from?" I said, "Ma I got them from you. I wrote them down on a little piece of paper.

Mom and the Eight Million Dollar Lottery Ticket

I was leaving the house and my father says to me, "You're a stupid. You quit a your job." I said, "Oh fuck, I just quit my job." I says, "I'm gonna call him up. My father says, "You gonna call this guy up? You just tell him to stick the milk and the sour cream up his wife's ass and now you're gonna call him up?" " I need to call him up. I need my job back."

So I call him up and I says, "Hey John." He says, "Who's this?" I said "Vinny." "You better stay the fuck away. If I see you I'll crack your fuckin' head open." I said, " Don't tell me he called you too." "What do you mean, he?" I said, "My cousin, he." John cut me off and said, "No listen to me. That was you!" I said, "My cousin sounds just like me. Got me in trouble with my wife, canceled my checks at the bank, I mean everything. He just totally fucked me up. His voice, he sounds just like me." "That was you, you shithead." I said "Listen. I could prove to you that that wasn't me." "How the fuck you gonna prove it?" "Calm down I told him, calm down. Now go look at the books. You owe me $310." "Hold on a second." He came back on the phone and said, Yeah $310, and that fuckin' guy sounds just like you." I said, "Would I quit if you owed me $310? When I get hold of him I'm gonna break his fuckin' head. He's nuts, he's crazy."

So I got my job back.

The phone bill was $29.

Who's Better Than You!

I had to wait a month and I paid the phone bill.
I was allowed to go back in the house.

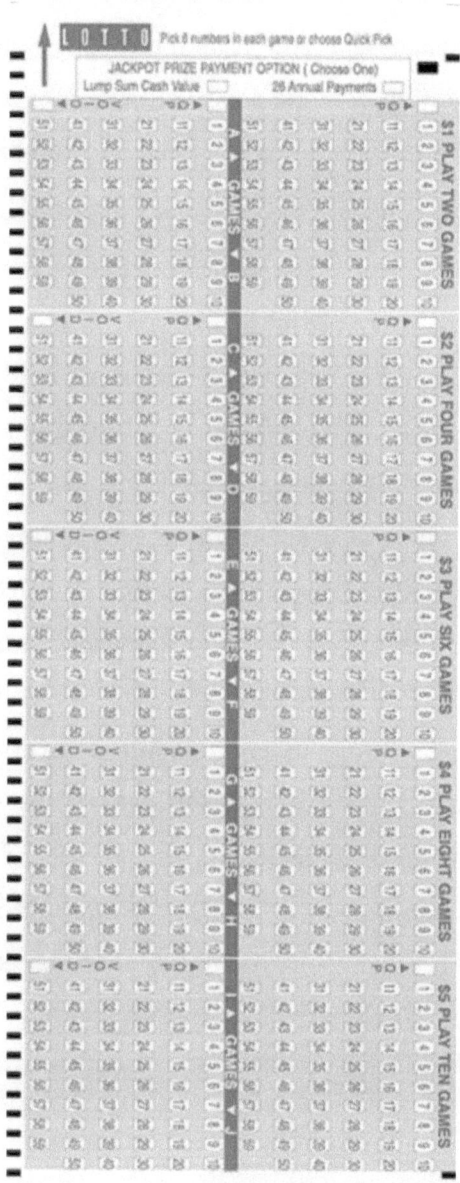

CHAPTER 22

WHATEVER YOU DO DON'T TOUCH IT, THEY'RE GONNA FIX

Now here I am in the 1970s and I was transporting a Honda Scooter from the Bronx to Manhattan for a friend of mine. Where did he get the scooter from? Well as I understood it, it happened to "fall off a truck."

So I'm going down Fifth Avenue somewhere in the 70-something streets, around two o'clock or three o'clock in the morning. I'm involved in an accident. Not my fault. It turns out that one of the owners of a major clothing men's store or someone who worked for them, was switching lanes or something. He hit me from behind and knocked me right off the bike. I flew up in the air and came down hard.

I sort of dozed off for a while. All I remember was the EMS guy was above me and they took me to Lenox Hill Hospital because the hospital was right there. I remember I was falling asleep on the X-ray table and the nurse said, "We might have to admit you because we might have to run more tests on you." I said, "Okay fine." I thought I didn't get hurt too bad. I got two stitches under my cakes.

Now it's around 5:30 in the morning, I wake up and I'm in what they called traction. I have a brace around my neck and my hands were to the side and the machine was pulling me. So I started pushing the button to get the nurse. The nurse came in and said, " Hi Mr. Vella. How are you feeling?" I said, "I guess I feel okay but what's all this stuff that I am in." I am not familiar with medical terms, so when she told me what I had, I didn't know what she was talking about. She said, "You have a fractured coccyx." So when she said that I had a fractured coccyx my eyes popped out of my head, I didn't know what it was. I thought it was a nice way of saying something else. So I looked at her and said. 'Will I ever be able to use it again?" She went "Ha, ha Mr. Vella, you're funny, you know where it is." I said, "I know where it was before I got here." So I start moving it around so I know it's okay. So she said, "Well you're sitting on it, honey. I have to leave now." I said, "Don't leave me and she said, "I'll be back."

So, when I tried to get out of bed, I realized what it was. It was the ass bone. I also found it out from somebody else.

So now I had to call my mother after spending two or three days in the hospital. I called her and she said, "Where are you,

Whatever You Do Don't Touch It, They're Gonna Fix It

you sonamabitch? I've been calling you for three days now. Where are you? What happened?" I said, "You're not going to understand this, I got into an accident." "What kind of accident?" I said, "A motorcycle accident." "What you do to yourself?" I said, "Let me explain, it's not what you're gonna think." She said, "Listen to me, I know everything about the doctor 'cause I go all the time." I said, "This is not what you're thinking it is. It's not in the front, it's in the back." "What's a not in the front, it's in the back? What the hell are you talking about?" "That's what I'm trying to tell you. That's what I got wrong, it's the ass bone." "What's a the ass bone that's not in the front that's in the back?" "Ma what I got is a fractured coccyx." "Oh my God! Here, tell a your father. She's going, "Louie, Louie hurry up he break a his thing, he's a broken his thing!" My father says, "Vinnie what did you break?" I said, "Pop she doesn't understand." My father said, "I understand it better than your mother, I go to the doctor all the time." I said, "That's what she said. Listen I was in a motorcycle accident and this is not in the front it's in the back." "What's a not in the front it's in the back? "he said. "It's the ass bone. Pa I got a fractured coccyx." He goes, "O my God! Listen I still love a you. I'm no ashamed of you. Whatever you do, don't touch it, they're gonna fix."

They didn't understand it.

Who's Better Than You!

So finally I was in the hospital for three or four days and I really realized what a fractured coccyx was. I tried to get out of bed. Oh man, did it hurt. I couldn't even sit down to pee. I had to go over the toilet like sideways trying to pee.

CHAPTER 23

WHAT A DRAG

Years ago it had to be in the sixties. I was working for this company called Zampieri Brothers Bakery. I was driving a truck delivering bread. It was a part-time job early in the morning. I would leave the bread in front of the doors of the stores in the neighborhood.

On the corner of 8th Street and 6th Avenue, they used to have all the drag queens and the hookers hanging out early in the morning. There was one over there, to me that was a woman. I mean there is no way it could have been a man. So beautiful. She used to say hello to me every morning, every time I would pass with the truck.

So one day I stopped.

Make a long story short I brought her on the truck with me, made a few stops, and started making out with her. I put my hand underneath her skirt and I felt something that I wasn't expecting. And I said, "Oh! Hold on a second. Are you a guy?" She said, "Yeah."

Who's Better Than You!

Well, I picked up a stale loaf of bread and I was beating him with a stale loaf of bread. I chased him up Greenwich Avenue. I was throwing bread and rolls at him. I couldn't catch him. I couldn't chase him too far, maybe about a block, block and a half 'cause I had the truck open, had bread in there, and all my personal belongings.

He's running up the block with his high heels on, screaming. You know it didn't make me look too good. So I figured you know what, I'll catch him again one of these mornings. Never seen him again.

But I have to say one thing he was beautiful though.

Not my type.

But beautiful.

CHAPTER 24

JOE RIGANO

Joe Rigano and I go way back and are great friends. I love the guy to death. In *Casino*, he's the guy with the raspy voice. We were in the movie *Coffee and Cigarettes, Ghost Dog* and other movies.

In *Casino*, I was the Underboss of Kansas City. He was the guy that said to me, (Vinny imitates Joe Rigano's rough voice) "Hey did you get to Vegas to get the money."

Well I am not goofing on him, but he had throat cancer. Sometimes I had a lot of fun with him. Now sometimes when he speaks he doesn't realize his lips will continue to move, but no sound comes out. So one day he was where I live and he goes, "Hey Vinny if I park my car around the corner do you… (Vinny imitates Joe making sounds, but no words come out). I said, "Joe your lips are moving, and no sound is coming out." Joe said, "Would you pay attention you fuckin' asshole." I said, "I did paid attention, your lips are moving, huh, what?" "Joe started again and said, "I park my car on… (Vinny imitates Joe making sound, but no words) and then says, "ticket". I said, "Joe, write it on a piece of paper." So he would get mad at me and he said, "Vinny go fuck yourself."

So now we're doing this event in Rhode Island. We went to do an appearance. So they put us on a gondola. We were in a bay and we had to pull up to a pond with all these people waiting for us. Just an appearance, signing autographs, and all that. After we got off the gondola this guy says, "Is there any way we can get you guys to do a speech." So I said, Let him do it first."

We're up on stage. He was so funny. He says, "You know I love Rhode Island. The last time I was here…(Vinny making unintelligible sounds imitating Joe with no words coming out until finally the word "great"). Now, I used to goof around on Joe all the time and when he was talking all of sudden he was standing right next to me and I just turned around to face him. I was staring at his mouth. He said, "Hey what the fuck are you looking at." Now all of a sudden he started to talk and he's telling a story up there. The lips are moving, and no sound came out. And I couldn't wait till he finished. Then when he finished (Vinny imitates Joe) "You tell 'em now, you tell 'em." He's telling me in other words now you can speak. I looked at the crowd and I said, "Anybody understand what the fuck he just said?" Oh man, fuckin' people were hysterical and they said, "Ah you're fuckin' crazy." Joe says, "Hey Vinny, go fuck yourself." We looked like fuckin' Abbott and Costello up there. It was fuckin' funny.

Now it got to the point when we had to do the voiceovers for the movie *Casino*. I went home, and they called me up from the movie and said, "Hey Vinny is there any way we can get you to come back in here tomorrow?" I said, "Did I make a mistake?" "No, no." "So what is it all about?" "Well we don't want to talk about it over the phone, so come down." So I went down there, and they said, "We had Joe down here to do one, but it's not coming out right. We know that you do a great imitation of him. Could you just say these two lines?" "Sure." "But please you can never tell him, you'll get us in a jam." I said, "Okay fine." So I did the two lines. When we were sitting down watching the screening Joe said, "Hey we did good heh." I said to myself, "Yeah that's my fuckin' voice up there." I didn't tell him, and I always used to bust his chops.

If you get to watch *Hey Vinny*, there's a part in it when you think he's talking, then all of a sudden the camera goes to him and you see he's not talking, it's me. It's identical.

Oh man, do I have a good one. We had this guy Stanley Kaplan he was our Manager, Jewish guy. When we were doing all the ESPN commercials he said, "Oh Vella I'm happy that you stopped over." He said, "Tomorrow morning I'm gonna meet you and Joe Rigano, we'll go to the set together. I'm gonna come to the set with you guys. So I got to let Joe know." I said, " I'm getting ready to go see Joe now. No, don't worry I'll tell him, and I'll have him call you later." I left. About fifteen minutes later I called up Stanley (Vinny talks to Stanley imitating Joe Rigano's voice) I go, "Hello Stanley." Stanley says, "Hi Joe." (Vinny still imitating Joe's voice) "What's this going on? I heard the thing was canceled. Heard everything was canceled." Stanley says, "Canceled?" "Yeah, Vinny Vella said tomorrow is canceled." Kaplan goes, "That fucking moron told you it was canceled? I told him to tell you to come here tomorrow morning at 10:30." So I says, (Vinny is no longer imitating Joe but speaking in his own voice) "You called me a fucking moron!" Stanley says, "Who is this?" I says, "Vella." He goes, "Put Joe back on the phone." Well of course I couldn't and he got wise to me.

So later when Joe calls him up, Stanley goes, "Vella, I got no time for you," and he keeps hanging up on Joe. Joe calls me up and says, "I'm calling Stanley from out on Long Island, and he keeps hanging up on me. He thinks it's you all the time."

Joe called me up and says, "Do me a favor leave that Jew bastard alone, he keeps fucking hanging up on me, thinks it's you."

Then we had this other guy. I did another imitation of another guy his name was Ray Serra. He died a number of years ago. I got Joe again.

I had two telephones. I called up Joe imitating Ray Serra's voice and said, "Hey Rigano this is Ray Serra, listen do me a favor. I have some guy told me to reach out to ya. Wants to use you in this movie." Joe says, "Yeah, yeah okay." I continued as Serra and say, "But whatever you do you can't tell your friend Vinny Vella or whatever his name is." "No, no, no. I ain't gonna say nothin'."

So now I'm calling him up on the other phone as Vinny and Joe goes, "Yeah, hello who's this?" I said, "It's me Vinny." He tells Serra who is me on the other line and says, "Hold on Ray, hold on one second." So I get on the phone as Vinny and I say, "Hey Joe." He goes, "Hey listen I can't talk right now I'm on the phone with my daughter." I said, Oh, "I'll call you later."

Meanwhile, I hang up and I get back on the other phone as Serra and Joe says, "What do they want me to do?" "They want you to walk into this social club, like a bar, the camera is gonna be in back of ya. They're not going to see a thing. Your pants got to be very loose, you got to hold them in the front and as your walking past this table with these wiseguys over there. Then your gonna let go of your pants, your pants are going to fall down, the guys gonna smack you in the ass, you pick up your pants and you walk out." "I don't know if I wanna do that." "Hey, listen to me, they told me to reach out to ya, the camera is gonna be in back of ya, they're not gonna see your face. They're gonna pay you three hundred dollars for ten minutes work." Joe says, "I really don't want to do it." Serra says, "What am I supposed to do, what am I supposed to tell these people?" Joe says, "You know what? Call Vinny Vella." So Joe didn't take the job.

Joe calls me back and says, What are you doin' Vinny? I tell Joe, "These people just called me up for a job." Joe says, "Oh I'm the one that told them to call ya." I said, "Yeah." Joe says, "What do you got to do, drop your pants? I said, "What?" Joe said, "What do they want you to do?" I said, "They want me to walk into this social club where there are going to be these wiseguys sitting down at the table. They want me to pull out a gun, shoot them in the head, drop the gun like they did in *Godfather*, and walk out. They're going to pay me $1500." "Wait, wait, hold on a second. What do they want you to do?" "They want me to walk into the club…" Joe says, "You got to drop your pants?" "Drop my pants, what are you talking about?" "They just called me up these motherfuckers, they wanted me to drop my pants. They were going to pay me $300." "I told them to call you and they're going to give you $1500? You got these fuckin' people; you got their fuckin' numbers?" "Yeah." I had a bunch of phones so I gave him one of the numbers. So Joe calls up and says, "Who'd I talk to before about the role and the show?" I said, "Hey Joe it's me, Vinny I was the one that called you before." Joe was pissed. "Stop fuckin' around. One of these days someone is gonna break your fuckin' head."

I even got his wife. Now if I could fool his wife you know I'm good. He's in the City and I am not with him. I know he's leaving to go home, so I call up his wife as Joe, and say, "Hello Marie," She says, "Hiya Joe." "Yeah, I'm still in the City with Vinny Vella. I'm going to catch a bite, and have a drink, I'll be home later." Marie said, "What are you talking about, you got your daughter coming over, you got your grandchildren…" As Joe, I said, "Yeah I know, make up an excuse for me." She goes, "Can't you see that moron some other time." So I said, "Hello Marie," She goes, "Hello." I said, "Marie it's me, Vinny." I hear her banging the phone and she says, "I don't know what happened. I just had Joe on the other line." I said, "No Marie that was me." She said, "I don't appreciate that, you asshole. Don't do that no more."

Nobody has a sense of humor.

I was just a joker that fucked around with everybody from day one.

Who's Better Than You!

CHAPTER 25

I JUST WON $5 MILLION IN THE LOTTERY

Here I am, I bought a lottery ticket, a $20, $500 Million Extravaganza New York Lottery ticket.

I buy it and I scratch it off and if you match any numbers on the top and the numbers on the bottom match, that's what you win. I bought it on Mulberry Street right off Prince Street in a bodega. This Arab guy, the owner was in there and anytime I bought a ticket for $20 he would give me two of them for $20. He would go partners with me, so if I win, he's my partner and if he wins, I'm his partner.

So the first ticket I'm scratching off. He's behind the counter and he said, "Did ve vin? Did ve vin?" In other words, did we win? So all of a sudden, I said, "Look at this we won $40." So we each got our $20 back.

So the second ticket I'm scratching off, 7 on the top and 7 on the bottom and when I looked underneath it said $5 MILLION! I got shortness of breath and my legs were getting weak on me and he's behind the counter saying, "Did ve vin? Did ve vin?" I have to be honest with you my legs buckled up under me and I had to catch my breath. I said "Come over here. Look we just won 5 MILLION DOLLARS!" He went, "5 MILLION DOLLARS!" He looked at the ticket. He looked at me. We are in the middle of Little Italy, he starts doing a dance and he said "Mu halla halla", mu halla halla," or something like that. I did not know what the hell he was saying, and I said, "Shut the fuck up with your mu halla, mu halla shit. People know me around here, you fuckin' jerk. Stop with your halla, halla shit." When he was busy yelling that he won the 5 million dollars people who were on line to buy something said, "Fuck him" and they were walking out with loaves of bread, bottles of soda, candy, and whatever they had. He wasn't interested in what they were doing. All he was concerned about was he just won two and a half million dollars. It was a Friday so I called the Lotto office and they told me it was a little too late to come into the office and I could come back Monday.

So I called up my wife and she was working in an after-school program. She never believes anything I say. I call her up and say, "Honey", and she says, "You know better than to call me up at the after-school program. What is it?" I said, "You're not going to believe this, I just won 5 MILLION

I Just Won $5 Million in the Lottery

DOLLARS!" She says, "Are you in the bar?" I said, "No I'm not. I just won 5 MILLION DOLLARS!" She goes, "Are you out of your fucking mind? Leave me alone I'm working," and she hung up on me. I said to myself, I'm going to call her again and if she fucking hangs up on me again, I'll be on unsolved mysteries, she won't get nothing.

She knew about the lottery thing with my mother so that's why she didn't believe me. She turned around and told her mother who was helping her at the time. She said to her mother, "I don't believe this son of a bitch won 5 million dollars." Her mother said, "Don't believe him, he did it to his mother"!

I called her back and I say, "Stop fucking hanging up on me. I just won 5 Million Dollars! Listen, I'm in the bodega on Mulberry Street between Prince Street and Spring Street. I bought a $20 Extravaganza ticket; you have to come here right away." She goes, "If this is a joke and if you didn't win, I'm going to stick that ticket up your ass." "I'm tellin' you, you can stick the ticket up my ass. I just won 5 MILLION DOLLARS! You can quit your job!"

So when she comes in there she sees the ticket and she got weakness in her legs like I did, and almost fainted. My friend had to hold her up.

That weekend my wife went to Cartier; she bought the Cartier watch she always wanted. She went to Tiffany's and she bought a little pendant. She bought airline tickets, first class. She booked rooms at the Fontainebleau Hotel. She did everything. Probably ran up a tab of about $22,000. I said, "What the fuck are you doing? "She said, "You cheap bastard you just won 5 Million fuckin' dollars! I can't spend a few dollars?" I said, "Wait till I have the money in my hand. Fuckin' spending all that money. "Are you crazy?"

So now I was a millionaire overnight, but by the time I went back Monday morning to go claim the ticket at the Lottery Office, I've already had like a million dollars spent. So when I got there, and they were scanning the ticket, the guy looks at me and I see him from behind the window give it to someone else. Then there was the third person who said that it was not coming up. Everybody had that look of doubt. They're looking at me and they're shaking their heads and putting their two hands up and I said, "I hope there's no problem with this friggin' ticket." Then about three or four more people come over and looked at the ticket. Finally, a guy comes over to me and says "I'm sorry but this ticket is not coming up a winning ticket. I said, "What are you talking about?" He said, "Well there is some sort of mistake here." I said, "There is a 7 on the top and a 7 on the bottom. If it looks, walks, and quacks like a duck, it's a fuckin' duck! I want my fuckin' money!" So they came up with, it's a misprinted ticket. My wife told Halla

Halla, the bodega owner who was with us, "Let's get out of here, you don't know him he's crazy."

I was fuckin' pissed off. I was disappointed. I didn't know what the fuck to do so I called my friend Larry at the New York Post newspaper and told him about it. He had them write it up. TMZ and other news outlets covered it. So I have to get a lawyer and other stuff. I went through four lawyers. The first three lawyers, one was a Jew, then a Jew, and then a Jew. One was worse than the other. Then I got this greaseball and he was worse than all of them. You know, you can't fight the judges because when you go to the court with something like this, you're fighting the city and the state. You're not gonna win. You got a better chance of seeing hell freeze over.

So I said, you know what, you're going to represent yourself. So when I was down there at the court, I told them, "I am going to represent myself." They said, "You need an attorney to represent you." I saw I couldn't win that argument so they gave me a Legal Aid Attorney. Now I had to wait another three hours.

A guy comes down and he begins to talk. I said, "I don't believe this! What am I on *Candid Camera* over here? Is this some kind of joke? Is this a continuation of *My Cousin Vinny*?" The guy was stuttering when he went in front of the judge, and he goes "Yourrrrrrrrrrrrrrrrrrrrrrrrr honor." I looked at him and I said, "I don't believe it!" I looked at the guy and I said, "You've got to be kidding me." I said, Are you serious?" Then he got mad at me. I said, "Would you speak up, I want to get out of here!" So then I started to talk, and the judge says, "Let your attorney speak for you," and I said, "The guy can't talk, he's freakin' stuttering, there is something wrong. I have been here four times with four lawyers. I have this one that stutters, you know I want to come to an end with this."

So the judge looks at the ticket and says, "I grant you twenty dollars." I say, "Twenty dollars? The judge says, "Yeah that was the cost of the ticket, right?" I said, "Yeah." The judge goes, "Do you have a problem with that?" I was so pissed off I said, "Yeah, you can stick the $20 up your wife's ass!"

So I got arrested on top of that. The next thing you know they take me in the back and the cops are taking pictures of me with their cell phones and I walk by this cell with all these black guys in there and they are saying, "Hey man, you're a star, they can't hold your ass in there." I said, "Are you going to put me with these guys here?" So the cop said, No we're going to put you in the back, and he says, "Can I call you Vinny?" I said, "Yeah." So he says, "Vinny are ya hungry?" I said, "Yeah." So he goes "All we have are bologna sandwiches." I said, "I don't eat that shit, I never ate that shit when I was in school, I ain't hungry. I got money on me; can you go outside and get me a hero sandwich and maybe a bottle of beer or something?" So he says, "Vinny we can't do that."

I was back there for a little while, then the cop comes back, and he says, "You know if you don't apologize to the judge they're gonna give you ten days." I was so pissed off I said, "You want to know something. If he could get me away from my wife for ten fuckin' days it might be a fuckin' blessing." I said, "You know what, tell the judge he can screw his wife or his boyfriend in Macy's window. I'm not going to apologize and tell him I said to go fuck himself. Let him know if he don't let me out of here, I've got a television show and I'll bad mouth him, and the Lottery Board. I'll go to every newspaper and every radio station show. You'd better get me the fuck outta here 'cause now I'm getting pissed off!"

I was there for another two hours. The cop finally came back and said, "Vinny listen, they're gonna let you out. Do me a favor when you pass by the judge please don't even look at him, don't look at him." I wanted to give that judge the finger so bad.

Then as I was leaving I'm thinking, that fucking bitch ran up a tab on me now. She spent all this fuckin' money. Cartier watch, Tiffany pendant, first-class airline tickets and the Fontainebleau Hotel. Well, to make a long story short I'm still paying the fuckin' thing off. I pay about $300 to $400 a month. But she just doesn't fuckin' learn and she keeps calling me a cheap bastard. "Why are you calling me a cheap bastard? You're the one that's wearing the fuckin' Cartier watch." I had to take the vacation because it was already paid for. What the fuck, I'm in a hole now for $22,000. So I paid off some of it.

So I wind up the thing with twenty dollars, the cost of the lottery ticket. The Lottery Board also admitted that the people that printed up the tickets had a problem with the ink. They had a problem with the ink! I didn't have no fuckin' problem with the ink! I should have been at least compensated more than twenty dollars. They ain't gonna give ya nothing and let me tell you this lottery thing is a bunch of horseshit 'cause to win the $5 million, you know what the odds are? They are 1 in 290 million to hit. You ain't gonna hit it. Maybe for every 10 tickets you buy, you might get your $20 back or you might get $40. You ain't gonna win. That's a business. They're there to make money, not give you money. All this is like Atlantic City and other stuff, it's a big racket.

All I ended up with was a Lottery t-shirt, a Lottery coffee mug, and a Lottery small cooler which I later broke up on a TV show.

So I had to return some of the stuff I bought with my "winnings", but that's another story.

Who's Better Than You!

CHAPTER 26

THAT'S THE MOST BEAUTIFUL GIRL I'VE EVER SEEN

The business I had was Star Truckers. They were recreational vehicles, those big Winnebago's, big RVs. We used to supply them out to the fashion industry, VH1, MTV, and sometimes movie sets. My partner's name was Phil Bleeth, and his daughter's name was Yasmine Bleeth, the one from *Baywatch*.

So there were so many incidents that I've run across. I did this for a good 15 years. There were these clients with the rag on. I would put on the generator once we get to the location. It would supply all the energy for the vehicle for hair, makeup, wardrobe, ironing, coffee, and a computer.

So one day as soon as we got on the vehicle and this woman said, "Do you have coffee?" She was a French woman. I said, "Yeah, but I can't make it till we get to the location." "Why not?" "I just told you I can't make it till we get to the location; it will spill all over the place."

So when we got there, she says," Do you have coffee?" I said, "Well I told you before we have coffee. We'll put it on now." So I am putting the water into the machine to make the coffee. She says, "How long does it take before the coffee comes out?" I said, "You know what, why don't you relax a little bit." I said, "If you're in a hurry for the coffee why don't you open up your mouth, put it underneath and when the coffee is coming out, I'll pour the sugar in your mouth." Well, that's all I had to say, 'cause she was such a bitch. So one of the wardrobe girls started to laugh. She says, "You are fired from listening to this idiot!" "Oh, you called me an idiot!" Then I said, "You know what, get all your shit off the vehicle." She says, "I am calling another vehicle. I don't want you anymore. You're fired!" I said, "I'm fired!" She says, "I will call another vehicle to come here and take your place." I said, "Meantime, I am not waiting for another vehicle to come. Get all your shit, take it off the vehicle." She said, "Why?" I said, "I'll take the vehicle back to the garage and you'll have to come over to the garage and get your stuff back over there." "You will wait!" she said. I said, "What? What are you, my mother?" I said, "I'm taking all that stuff back to the garage." I shut off the generator. I pulled the steps in from outside and started to go. She freaked!

That's the Most Beautiful Girl I've Ever Seen

I never told anybody that I was the owner, because if they ever complained and they said," You're the owner I want you to knock this off the bill." I then said, "I'm just the driver." We used to do that back and forth me and Phil. One time he was the owner, the next time the owner was on vacation, etc.

I used to hire drivers and they used to sit in front of the vehicle, and they would adjust the mirror so they could see the girls dressing and undressing in the back. I used to tell them, "Listen do me a favor, this is not a peep show, when the girls are undressing in the back you turn that mirror around or go outside the vehicle. Do not make them feel uncomfortable, that reflects on me, and they won't hire me anymore. Don't do it!"

I caught this guy once. He actually turned the chair around, faced them and he put sunglasses on. I said, "You got all your marbles up there or what? What are you doing?" "Oh, I'm sitting here." "Why are you facing this way? The girls are dressing, you know what. Outside!" "Outside," he said, "It's cold!" "You know what I don't give a fuck, put on your coat." I used to fire them left and right. Now whenever I was there and if it was cold I would sit in the front, turn the mirror, and face the front. I would do my paperwork. They all knew me and respected me for all that.

I'm sitting up front one day and they were shooting lingerie for Victoria's Secret. The models used to get prepared inside the vehicle. I am sitting down, and a girl comes over to me and she says, "Vinny can I have one of your cigarettes?" I was smoking at that time. I turned around and she was naked from the waist up. Right there. I looked at her tits and I said, "How ya doin'?" So yeah, back then I used to see a bunch of them and every day I said, "Wow, that's the most beautiful girl I've ever seen!" And the next day I would say, "No, no that's the most beautiful girl I've ever seen." But they were so beautiful, because when they came in, in the morning, they didn't have any makeup or nothing on, not even anything in their hair, they would just take a shower and dry their hair. They would do everything there, so they used to come on looking very pretty and then when they were all done up, sometimes you wouldn't even recognize them. So they'd be five-foot-nine and they'd be stepping out of the vehicle they would be like six-foot-one. They were just so beautiful and such nice girls. I used to fall in love every day. I really did and they liked me.

One time it was freezing outside and there were so many girls in the vehicle. They were dressing and undressing, so I'm putting on my scarf, and they said, "Where are you going?" I said, "I figure I'll step out of the vehicle, there are so many of you in here. I'll go find somewhere to stay warm." "You could stay here Vinny." I said, "Really I appreciate it but…" "We wouldn't want you to get sick, don't worry stay here." So

That's the Most Beautiful Girl I've Ever Seen

I did and they would call me in the back of the RV. They were all undressed. Then when the generator stopped working they would yell, "Vinny the generator." I had to go back and start it again because if you plug too many things into one side it generates insanity, you have to equal it out." Sometimes supplies would run low and I would hear,"Vinny, is there any more coffee, is there any more paper cups?" I had to pass all these girls with nothing on, but I would joke around with every one of them. I said, "Oh, I'm in heaven let me just find some cups", and they would laugh.

At a shoot one day there was this famous rapper who was our client. I was outside the vehicle talking to this cop who was a friend of mine. Meanwhile, the windows are wide open in the back of the vehicle. The marijuana smell and smoke was coming out. My friend goes, "What are they smoking in your vehicle?" I says, "I don't know." He went to the back and he opened up the door. They had all kinds of drugs laying out in there. He was starting to call for help. I said, "Please if you arrest these guys right now my day is going to be over with them and I got a long day. I'm making a lot of money with them over here. Could you give them a break and take all the shit and throw it all the fuck out?" He said, "Now first of all I don't like this guy." "I understand, but please give him a break, I don't like him either. But please give him a break otherwise I am going to lose a day."

He took all that shit, yes all that shit threw it away and told them, "If it wasn't for him, meaning me, I would have taken all of you in!" The cop leaves him alone and says, "I don't want to smell anything." He searched everybody; he searched the whole back of the vehicle.

Then all of a sudden after everything went down the rapper says to me, "Man they took everything, they took all of our shit." I said, "Yeah your right." "Man that's all we had; he took everything." I said, "You rather he take that, or you rather him take you to fucking jail?" "Man, you should have kept quiet man", he said to me. "I did you a favor and you're telling me to keep quiet!" For the rest of the day, they were spilling things all over the floor and making the place dirty.

I had Madonna on my vehicle. VH1 they gave out a carry-on bag that said VH1 on it. It was beautiful, the kind of carry-on you can carry all your suits or dresses. So this guy knocks on the door and said, "I got a gift for Madonna from VH1." I said, "I'll take it." He says, "I'm supposed to give it to her." I says, "I'm sorry I can't let you in the vehicle." He says, "Why not?" I said, "Because I'm not supposed to let you in the vehicle! I don't know who you are." "I just told you…" I said, "It doesn't matter, I have to watch Madonna to make sure nobody bothers her." I said, "Wait here a second." So I went

That's the Most Beautiful Girl I've Ever Seen

in the back, and I said, "Madonna I'm sorry to bother you." "Yeah, what is it, Vinny?" The guy over here is from VH1, he's got a carry-on bag and he wants to give it to you as a gift from VH1." "All right get it for me." I went back and I said, "She told me to get it for her. "He said, "Well I'm supposed to give it to her." Then I said, "You know what, keep it I don't want it." He said, "Would you make sure she gets it? "What do you mean make sure she gets it? Where am I in Central Park? "There's nobody here, she'll get it." So I brought it in, and I showed it to her and she looked at it and said, "You can keep it," and she gave it to me. So I ended up giving it away 'cause I didn't have any use for that.

I've worked with the very best of people. I worked with Frederique, from Victoria's Secret, Veronica Webb, Cindy Crawford, and Chris Turlington. Just so many models and I have pictures to prove it all. The models always used to say, "Can you hire that company with that Vinny Vella? I was busy as all shit.

I was always working.

Later on, my partner left the business and so did I.

Who's Better Than You!

Chapter 27

COCAINE AND CLOROX

There was this girl I met. She was a Puerto Rican girl. I met her in New York. After a while I had her move in with me. What happened was in those days I was dealing with a lot of cocaine. So what happened was I trusted her and I had cocaine all around the house. I had so much of it that if a little bit was missing I couldn't tell. Rocks you name it, whatever.

So one day she went out to have her hair done and I was looking for something and I went into her closet. I had a 2 bedroom apartment and I let her use one bedroom to put her own clothes in and her own stuff in there. She had everything packed in boxes in a corner of one of the closets. Everything was packed so nice.

So I decided when she went out to have her hair done, let me just take a look and see what she's got there. When I opened the boxes up, boy was I surprised. There had to be at least in weight maybe a 1/2 pound. That was a lot. You know back then it was like $1100, $1200, $1300 for a 1/2 pound back then. Now it's like nothing. And when I opened the boxes up I seen it and thought oh shit, that was all my stuff. So I repacked it exactly the same way.

When she came back from getting her hair done she asked me for some cocaine. I said, "You got plenty there in the closet." She said, "What are you talking about?" I said, "You got quite a bit of cocaine in that closet. Where did you get it all?" "Oh, it was mine, I had it for a long time." I said, "No, no, no, no, no! You didn't have it for no long time. You did not have that shit for a long time. That's mine. I recognize that fucking cocaine man. I recognize those rocks and everything else." So I told her I wanted her out of here. I took all the cocaine. I said, "That's mine, it's not yours, it's mine!"

She didn't want to go. So finally she started freaking out. So I said oh shit. So I didn't know what to do 'cause now she's freaking out in my house, I got a lot of cocaine in my house. So I told her, "You gotta leave." She says, "No it's mine, it's mine." I said, "No you think it's yours, it is mine."

So all of a sudden she started drinking Clorox. Don't ask me why, 'cause I don't know why. All of a sudden her eyes started going behind her head, she was like freaking out. I

Cocaine and Clorox

said, "I want you out of my freaking house." I had a lot of cocaine, a scale, screens, you name it. So I told her she had to leave. She said, "No, I no go no place, I love you." I said, "You don't love me, you steal from me. You gotta get the fuck out of here." So, finally, she was making all kinds of motions and started dancing wildly around my house. I said, Oh shit, she's freaking.

I called Carlos the doorman downstairs. I told him "You got to come up here right away!" He said, "What happened?" I said, "She drank Clorox and she's freaking out." He said, "No, no, no, no. Mr. Vella the washing machine is on the 4th floor." I said, "I don't want no washing machine you fuckin' idiot." He thought I was talking about the fucking laundry room. I told him, "You gotta call the cops because I can't help her. I can't have her up here."

When she was drinking the Clorox I said, "Put ice in it bitch, it will taste a lot better." I thought she was joking around. The Clorox was in a glass and she diluted it. So finally I let her lay on the floor. I was breaking up the scale, ripping the screen apart, putting cocaine in the toilet, you name it. I was cleaning up the house while she was dying. I didn't want the cops coming in the house because I had a house full of fucking cocaine.

So finally we came to the point where she was really

breathing heavily. I said, Oh no that's it, I'm fucked up now. So I called an ambulance, but I realized I had to drag her down to the lobby. I didn't want her to die in my fucking apartment. So when they came they said, "What happened? I said, "I don't know. She's passing out or something. I don't know what's wrong with her."

They took her away and I went to the hospital with her. She was still breathing heavily and she said, "I love you." I said, "You don't love me." I went to the hospital with her because I wanted to make sure what she was going to say. By then my house was like a church, there was nothing in it. I got rid of a couple of thousand dollars of coke easily between my own and hers. I had to get rid of everything.

I didn't know what they were doing to her, but they said she got a lot of cocaine in her system. They asked, "Has she ever done anything like that before?" I said, "I don't know." They said they smelled Clorox and asked, "Has she ever done that before? I said, "I don't know. She used to do the laundry a lot." I didn't know what to say. Finally I said, "The girl's nuts, maybe she didn't know what she was doing." So they were looking at me and I was looking at them.

I went back to the house, packed her clothes, and told her, "You got to go back to Puerto Rico. She said, "No." I said, "What do you mean no?" "I call the police," she said. "I don't

Cocaine and Clorox

care who the fuck you call, the house is clean. I got nothing in my house." She said, "I get you go to jail." I said, "I ain't going nowhere you fuck. You're going to Puerto Rico. You ain't staying with me you motherfucker."

She had been robbing me all the time. I also found money. It wasn't much, a couple a hundred bucks maybe.

I left her in the hospital. I didn't know what they did with her.

They must have straightened her out a little.

Never seen her again.

Who's Better Than You!

CHAPTER 28

YOU TRYING TO MAKE A MONKEY OUT OF ME?

Now my partner in the business, he did the mechanical work and the books. I used to work with the customers because he knew they all liked me.

So one day when I came to work and he said, "We got a new job tomorrow, a new client." I said, "I don't have a problem." He said, "Yes, but this one is going to be a little different. You're going to be picking up a monkey and a guy who is his owner and trainer." He said, "They're gonna use a monkey for this shoot, it's for this upscale clothing store." I'm thinking of a little monkey, the kind you would put on top of an accordion, like the one you see in the movies that would sit on their shoulder. "So when you get to Fifth Avenue and 16th St. I want you to pull the van up parallel to this guy's white van, knock on the door let him know you are there, then open up your door he'll come in with the monkey, and then you can drive them to the location."

Who's Better Than You!

So I drive to where the white van is, and I have to double park and I'm watching the back of the vehicle to make sure I don't get a ticket because my vehicle is double parked. I open the door. All of a sudden I feel something pulling my coat. I turned around and I jumped back four feet because I was afraid of this thing. It was a freakin' chimpanzee. I've never been that close to a chimpanzee. It had the underwear and the shorts and the sneakers, a baseball hat, and as soon as he looked at me he started doing all that monkey shit. He went HOO… HOO… HOO… HOO…with its teeth showing. I thought oh now I got to deal with this fuckin' thing and he was making me crazy. He looked at me and there was his teeth. He kept going HOO… HOO… HOO. So what am I going to do?

So now I'm facing the front of the vehicle cause I'm driving, and right behind me is the couch, and that couch is facing the passenger side of the vehicle. Now the fucking chimpanzee is sitting right behind me. So then I had to figure out what happened because that thing gave me a smack in the back of the head. BOOP! Now the guy, the trainer, was sitting alongside the monkey. So I figured the trainer saw his right hand go up, but then I figured out, that the little motherfucker was hitting me with his left hand. He was smacking me with the back of his hand. BOOP! That thing hurt. His hands were like freaking rubber.

You Trying to Make a Monkey Out of Me

So, I couldn't turn around right away because I was driving a 40-footer. So I said to myself I know I am fucked up, but this thing just slapped me. So by the time I turned around the monkey was sitting with his hands on his lap. His trainer was sitting next to him, and he was reading a newspaper. So I don't say nothing the first time. So I'm going down Fifth Avenue making a right turn on Ninth Street passing a place called Marylou's Restaurant, and we're headed west. BING! He gives me another slap. So once again I couldn't turn around. So I pulled over to the curb. The guy said, "Are we here?" I said to the guy, "No we're not here. You're reading the fuckin' newspaper and your fuckin' monkey keeps slapping me. Why don't you go in the back with him." The guy says, "He slapped you?" "Yeah, I said, "He slapped me twice. I am going to wind up in an accident. I almost went through the window this time." He said, "Hold on let me correct him. "Hobo, Did you slap him?" I said, "Hold on a second. You're going to ask the fuckin' monkey if he slapped me?" I said, "What are you trying to make a jerk out of me?" He says, "No he is very intelligent." I says, "Listen to me." I said, "I don't give a fuck how intelligent he is, I'm telling you he smacked me." "I believe you. I just want to correct him." He looks at the monkey and says, "Hobo did you slap him?" Hobo, shakes his head no, and behind the guy's back, I swear to my mother, he sticks out his tongue at me. I said under my breath, "You little motherfucker you."

So now I pull up to the location. They left Hobo alone with me. The first thing he did was to come over to me after the owner stepped out of the vehicle, and he jumped up, took my pen out of my pocket, and he threw it across the motor home. I didn't want him to see that I was pissed off because I figured he'd get the vibes and bite me, or something, or hurt me. So I just looked at him and said, "No you little shithead, you don't do that. That's a no-no." Then I turned around. The caterer comes in and they have fruit juice, bagels, and grapes. After the caterer left it took an orange and made a noise with its mouth and threw the orange at me. I caught it. I don't want to play catch with this thing. I don't want to bother with it. I said, "You don't do that you little motherfucker. No. Bad." I just wanted to do a job and that's it. I put the orange down and then he started throwing breadsticks at me. Then he came over to me with a handful of watermelon pits, hit me, and flipped them in my face.

So finally his owner comes back into the motorhome, and I said to him, "Can I speak to you for a second?" I said, "First of all he took my pen threw it across the motorhome, threw an orange at me, threw his breadsticks at me, now he's hitting me in the face with all the watermelon pits." He goes, "He likes

You Trying to Make a Monkey Out of Me

you." "He likes me. Let him like somebody else over there, there are 25 people over there. What do I look like his uncle or something? Let him be with somebody else for a half hour."

Now they took him out to use him for the shoot, so they harnessed him into a Jeep, but to keep him calm, they gave him a handful of grapes. So they made it very Safari-looking, and I'm standing where the photographer is, with a line of people. There must've been about 20 people watching this shoot. He's looking into the crowd with the grapes in his hand going, "HOO… HOO… HOO… HOO… HOO… HOO… HOO." And then he is looking around. I said to myself it looks like the son of a bitch was looking for someone. I stopped and I said, nah he ain't looking for someone, he's looking for me. "HOO…HOO...HOO…" He hit me right in the head with a grape. So everybody starts laughing. By that time I was kind of pissed off at this thing. I said to the owner, "You know what I don't live too far from here, I'm going to go home and get a gun and shoot this fuckin' thing." So everybody was saying they wanted to take pictures with this thing. I don't want to take pictures with this thing. I was afraid of it; I didn't want to be near it.

At the end of the shoot when the guy was leaving the motorhome, he went down the steps first with the chimpanzee right behind him, holding his hand. The chimpanzee gave me

Who's Better Than You!

a look like, Ha, ha, I had you all day long, I screwed you up or whatever. I didn't want him to think he had the best of me, so I put my foot out and I tripped him. Wow, did he got pissed off. He was trying to pull away from the guy and the guy said, "What happened?" I said, "I don't know he must have tripped on the steps; you'd better get him the fuck out of here. There is something wrong with this monkey."

I never saw Hobo again.

CHAPTER 29

CASINO

Let me tell you about being casted as a Wiseguy. I'm really a lover, not a fighter.

Here I was, I went down for the audition for *Casino*. I end up playing the Underboss of the Kansas City crime family.

Not only did I get the part, but Martin Scorsese's mother knew me because the building she used to live in, is the building I'm now living in. I remember when they all lived in the neighborhood there. So when she sees me she went, "Vinny what are you doing here?" I said, "I'm in the movie." "What movie?" *Casino*. "Who put you in?" I says, "Your son." She says, "Ah, he's a good boy." So I would hang around with her a little bit because I speak Italian, and she was such a beautiful, nice woman. So I guess in the past he used to see me hanging around with her and talking with her.

Now it came time for the scene and I'm on the set. I am the Kansas City boss Artie Piscano. Now, Martin Scorsese never writes his mother in prior to filming, he decides along the way.

Who's Better Than You!

He decides I'm going to put her in this scene, I'm going to put her in that scene. So what happened was he decided he was going to put her in a scene with me in a grocery store.

He says to me, "Every time you curse she's going to interrupt you and when she interrupts you, turn around and apologize to her. Remember where you left off and pick up from there." Whoa, it's easy for him to say. For me when you got all your lines down, and all of a sudden you're interrupted, and then you have to turn around and say something else and it's not in the script, and remember where you left off, it can be a little difficult. He says, "Is there a problem? "I says, "Well, I just want to make sure I'm able to do it cause I'm going to be distracted by your mother telling me not to curse and all that." He says, "Don't worry Vince if it don't work that way, we'll try something else." He used to call me Vince. Well, it really wasn't working. So he says, "All right listen, if someone owes you money and they don't pay you, what would you do?" "I'd break your freaking head." "That's what I want you to say. Now you got Nance that's screwing you up. You got the counting room that they won't even let you in. You got this one, you got that one, you got everyone against ya. I want you to say something about each and every one of em, and get down on every one of em, and show me how pissed off you are about all this stuff that's going on."

So I did and I went off. The guy who played my brother-in-law in the scene, George Comando was in shock because he had the script and all he had to say was, "You gotta lay down the law otherwise they're gonna make a fool out of you." He had the rest of the script in front of him. He knows what my lines are. And my lines were nothing compared to what he had on paper.

I said, "They're not gonna make a fool out of me. I write it all down in this book. Every fucking nickel, it goes down right here. Receipts, bills, everything's here." George is looking at me like, what's happening here, this is not in the scene, am I lost somewhere? Oh, man! I just kept rambling and rambling and rambling and Martin Scorsese was watching it on the TV monitor in another room. He said, "Just keep rambling till I say cut." I was running out of things to say. I didn't know what to say anymore and I just kept rambling and rambling.

And then all of a sudden he says, "Cut."

He comes out of the room with his hands on his head. I thought he was going to come over to me and say Vinny what the hell are you talking about? What are you saying? And he looked at me, came over to me, and put his two hands on my shoulders, and he said, "Perfect, that's exactly what I'm looking for. Now I want you to say it all over again. You remember what you said?" "What I said?" I didn't even know what the hell I said. He says, "Well then say something like that again, just keep going on. I want a camera over here, I want a camera over there, I want one up here." He had cameras all over the place. So just before he walked away, I said, "Marty can I ask you something please?" He said, "Sure Vince what is it?" I said, "When you like something that I do, do me a favor don't approach me with your hands on your head. I thought you were just going to send me home."

In the scene, his mother was a pisser because every time I cursed she would say something to me like, "Hey, oh, ah! What's the matter with you? Since when do you talk like that?" Then all of a sudden I said, "I'm sorry. Nance gives me trouble, and I'll tell him, screw around with those suitcases and I'll take the eyes out of his freakin' head." And again I said, "I didn't curse, I said 'freakin' head." She said, "Again!"I said, "I didn't curse, I said 'freakin' head." They're not gonna make a fool out of me. I write it all down in this book, every fuckin' nickel that goes down. Right here, receipts...," and we just kept going and going and I have had everybody tell me, "Vinny, you stole that scene."

Another memorable scene in the movie was when the FBI raided my house at the end of the movie. Marty says, "I want you to tell the FBI's guys something." So they're looking for the books and find them and they went, "Bingo we got him!"

Casino

And the FBI guy picks up the books out of the draw and he goes, "Hey we got 'em", and he's showing all the other FBI guys the books and he comes over to me and he goes "What's this Mr. Piscano? I said, "Those are not my books, those are my mother's books." He said, "Put the fucking cuffs on him" and I then dropped dead of a heart attack.

I'll never forget that my wife, the girl who played my wife. I was laying down on the floor with my legs open. She bent down to help me out and she hit me with her knee right in between my legs and I went ahhhhhhh!

I said, "Sweetheart, you're not supposed to be bringing me back to life. I'm supposed to die."

Who's Better Than You!

CHAPTER 30

YOU NEVER TOLD ME YOU WERE IN *SPIDERMAN*

There was this one time, I don't remember what movie it was that was filming while I was living on Elizabeth Street at the time. I went down to check the mail 'cause we used to get the mail very early in the morning. I came downstairs and they had all the barricades in front of my truck and my building. I only had a bathrobe on. This guy says, "Hey you're Vinny Vella. Are you in this movie?" "No, I live in this building, I come down to check the mail." He says, "Could you wait here a second?" I wound up getting a part in that movie. I don't remember what movie it was.

There was another time they asked me if I wanted to be in a movie when I came out of my building. I said, "No I can't I have to be uptown somewhere." Then I went into a candy store and came out on Bleecker Street and Carmine Street. I didn't look to see where the cameras were filming, and I started walking up the block. That day I had to meet my friend

Who's Better Than You!

Jimmy at John's Pizzeria and that's where I was going.

My sister calls me up about eight months later and she says, "You never told me you were in *Spiderman*." "*Spiderman*, I'm not in *Spiderman*." "No, no, no, it was you." "Are you sure? "You're Vinny, you're my brother, I know what you look like." People were calling me up and saying, "Hey Vinny you were in *Spiderman*. "Are you sure?" "Vinny we know what you look like, we've seen you coming out of the store and walking up the block." I had no idea; I didn't even know the name of the film was *Spiderman*. All I saw was a guy on the corner with the camera. That was it. So I had to rent the movie. There I am! Now I was gonna get my money back for the rental and more.

I called them up and I tell them, I said, "Listen, somebody came over to me and asked me if I wanted to be in the movie, I told them I was in a hurry and I couldn't do it, so I left. The next thing you know I was in the movie." "What's your name?" "Vinny Vella." "What part?" I told him what happened again. He says, "Okay are you union?" I said, "Yes I am in the union." He said, "Well we'll send you a check for $125, that's what we pay for extra work." I said, "Listen to me, I don't do extra work." "That's all you did in the film." "You shot me without my permission. I didn't do any extra work, you're the one who shot me." I says, "I want principal

You Never Told Me You Were in Spiderman

pay for coming out of the store." He said, "Well we can't do that." I said, "You know what, then I'm going to sue you for putting me in the film."

They called me back and said, "They're gonna pay you principal, but you're not going to be on the credits." So I got $900 walking out of a candy store.

Who's better than you.

Who's Better Than You!

CHAPTER 31

WE'RE ALL LOOK-ALIKES

I went up to this event in upstate New York.

It had to be ten to fifteen years ago. It was supposed to be a fundraiser for children. We got a bunch of actors together. The arrangement from the girl we talked to was there is no pay, but she's going to limo us all out there. In addition, she'll put us in a hotel overnight, with free food and all this other stuff and then we'll be chauffeured back the next day. We all figure we'll go up there and have a goof. So we had a bunch of actors in the car, not big-time actors, but guys you would know from movies they were in. One guy couldn't show, so we got this guy Mario. Mario is a Joe Pesci look-alike and sound-alike to fill in.

We went up there and got dropped off to this big mall before we got ready to go to the fundraiser. The event was going to take place in an open field. There were all these markets out there. There were these stands where you could buy food. When we were in the mall, Mario aka Joe Pesci is signing autographs. He wrote, "I love your perfume, when can I see you again." He signed the autograph, Joe Pesci.

All of a sudden, oh wait the best part was when we got up there in the limo. All of a sudden, we're in the limo and the car is jumping all over the place bump, bump, bump, bump. Where the fuck are we? I'm looking out the window and all I see is woods on both sides of the place. I said, "Where the hell are we?" All of a sudden we get out of the car, and it was like one of those places where they ring the big triangle, and everyone eats together. So I got out of the car, and I looked at this place. It was a dump! It had a stupid name something like the Tomahawk Inn or something like that. I am looking at this place and this woman comes over to me with a clipboard and she goes, "And who's Vince Villa? I said, "Not Vince Villa, Vinny Vella." She said, "You get the Villa here." I said, "This place has got a Villa? Come on you got to be kidding me. What kind of place is this?" She says, "The Villa is on the other side of the field, a little house over there, but the hotel is over here and all the rest of you are going to be over there at the hotel." "Why do I have to go over there?" She goes, "Because you're going to get the Villa." "How do I get there, I got luggage." She says, "Oh you can just walk right through." It was like grass about 2 1/2 feet high. "I gotta walk

We're All Look-Alikes

through this? Nobody carries luggage around here. You got to be kidding me. You know I don't want to stay there. I want to stay with my friends over there at the hotel." What a fucked up thing that was.

So we go back to this mall at night. There he goes signing things again. "I love you, Joe Pesci." "I like your perfume, Joe Pesci." So just before we are ready to go from the mall to the open market, this girl comes back and she goes to Mario, "Excuse me I just found out you're not the real Joe Pesci! Why would you sign Joe Pesci?" And he starts to leave, shrugs his shoulders, then walks away, and leaves her with me. She goes, "How rude of him. What an asshole."

Now I'm there with the guy who played Frankie Coffeecake in *A Bronx Tale*. His name is Dave Salerno. She turns to me and says, "What do you have to say? I said, "I happen to be a real actor." "Oh yeah. What were you in?" I said, "Did you ever see the movie *Casino*? She goes, "Oh yeah, I loved that movie." Now anyone should know, if you have some common sense, you seen the girl is upset, keep your mouth shut! David Salerno who is still there goes, "Oh come on tell her, we're all look-alikes." And the girl looked at me and she went, "Fuck off man." I turned to David Salerno and said, "Aww you fuckin' jerk you, why did you tell her that for?"

Nobody showed up for this fundraiser. Nobody. It was embarrassing. So this woman that was running the whole thing came over to us. I say to her, "What's going on? She says, "Nobody wants to come, they all think youse are all lookalikes." I turned to David Salerno and said, "You see what you started over here you moron!"

Now, I didn't want to stay in that hotel no more because there were like these little animals hanging on the doorstep looking at me as I walked into the room. I guess it was a couple of praying mantises. I could have swore I seen something run by me into the room. I got out of that room really quick.

So we checked out of the ridiculous fundraiser we get in the car and went over to the nearby Holiday Inn.

After we checked in we said what the fuck and went into the bar to hang out for laughs and drinks. It just so happened that David Salerno knew the owner of this hotel. The owner comes over and she goes, "David, what are you doing here? He says hello to her and says, "We're up here for a fundraiser and blah, blah, blah, blah blah blah." She says, "I have my Comedy Club in here. Please I would love for you guys to come into the Club here tonight."

She puts us at a table right in the front of the stage. The first one to come up to the stage was this girl. She comes up and starts her routine. It was embarrassing. She is up there imitating a chicken. "Buck, buck, buck, buck, buck, buck" and nobody was paying any attention to her. And she kept looking at me. And I didn't want to be like disrespectful. I was embarrassed for her. Oh no it was unbelievable. She was only up there for five minutes. There was this setup with signals, green, yellow, and red. First, you get the green light, that means you talk. When you see the yellow light come on, you got three minutes left. Then when the red light comes on that means you're done.

After Buck Buck got off the stage I was like, oh shit, this is a comedy club and David's friend owns it, and people are getting up and walking out. Everybody's talkin', nobody's paying any attention to the comedians. Then another guy gets up there. What an idiot! He started saying all kinds of jokes. Nobody was paying any attention to him either. And I'm sitting right in the front and again I didn't want to be disrespectful.

Meanwhile, David is talking to the owner, "You should get this guy Vinny Vella up there, he's funny. It'll hold your crowd, this that, and this that." She comes over to me where I am at the table with five or six people and she goes, "Excuse me, David was telling me that you're really funny. We have people walking out of the club right now. We'd like to have them stay. Is there any way I can get you to go up there?" I said, "Ahhh, no not really." I said, "I am not ready for it. For me to get up there I have to be drunk on Grand Marnier." She said, "I'll put a bottle of Grand Marnier on this table, and nobody gets a check." All my friends said, "Vinny, you better get the fuck up there." I said, "Ah man, you know what I want. I want an introduction. I want somebody to go up there and introduce me. I'm not just going to go up there without an intro because nobody is going to pay any attention to me. I want an introduction and it's gotta be said the way I'm gonna tell it to them. It needs to be "Vinny Vella from *Casino* from this, from that, buh, buh, buh, buh."

So, when I got up there, wow it was quiet, and I started with some of my stories. People were saying to the people who were walking out, "Hey you, come on, you gotta come back in here, look at this guy they got." All of a sudden all those lights went off, in other words, like you stay up there. I was up there for a good fuckin' half hour, forty minutes until the red light finally came on. Ah man, when I was finished people were buying us drinks and sending bottles over to the table. The owner came over to me and offered me a job. "If you come up here, five hundred dollars if you come up every weekend." I said, "I can't go for that."

I had one guy who laughed so hard when I told the coccyx story, well, he was choking on something. All of a sudden they went behind him and started giving him the Heimlich Maneuver. Everything stopped. He was facing the stage then something flew out of his mouth. I said, "You all right?" It went right past me on the stage. I said, "He must be all right by now." He had tears coming out of his eyes, he was curled up in a ball. His wife said, " In four years that I am married to him I never seen him laugh so fuckin' hard."

So I had a ball up there, you know. I didn't get nothin' for it, I mean we didn't get no check at the table. She wanted to know if we'd come in the following night. I said, "We're leaving in the morning."

We never did the fundraiser that night.

Who's Better Than You!

CHAPTER 32

NICKNAMES

Frank Aquilino got his name "Butchie The Hat" because ever since he was a kid, he always wore a hat. He was in a bunch of movies. *Analyze This, Goodfellas,* and *Analyze That.* So he's been around a lot. A good friend of mine. He hangs out here at La Mela's restaurant and he lives right around the corner. We call him "Butchie The Hat" because he always wears a hat. Never takes the hat off. The only time he takes his hat off is if he has to go to a funeral.

But Italians are the worst. God forbid if somebody should lose an eye or lose a leg or they become a hunchback. If this happened to any other nationality they would say, "God be with that person." Not Italians. If a guy loses his finger they say, "There goes 'Joey Thumb'." Or if a guy loses an eye they say, "Look there's 'Frankie Eyes'." They make up all these nicknames for people that have been hurt. They're crazy. Only Italians would do something like that.

I heard "Augie Apples" as a nickname. This guy used to

go upstate all the time and rob fruit and vegetables off of these farmers. He'd come back with carloads of fuckin' fruits, vegetables, and watermelons and sell them. They named him "Augie Apples." He had a business! He was robbing all that shit upstate. Every other day he would come back with carloads of corn, lettuce, and watermelons in a little van. He jumped over fences and grabbed all he could fit in his van. He had a nice business. Finally, we heard that Augie got busted because all the farmers were looking for this cocksucker for the longest time. He winds up like doing six months in jail.

Then there was Joey Beans. Got his name because he used to fart all the time. The fuckin' people are nuts.

Here is another one. There was this building, it was only two stories high, and this guy he pushed this other guy off the roof. There were these piles of garbage, and nothing ever happened to the guy, he survived. The guy who pushed him thought he had killed him. So it ends up that the guy landed in the garbage and the guy who pushed him took off. I don't know where he went, he left the state. Fuckin' went to Mississippi, went to California, went somewhere. He was gone for six months. He finally found out nothing ever happened to the guy he pushed off the roof, and that the guy was still walking around. So they named him "Bobby Balls." Why did they call him Bobby Balls? Because he had balls, he pushed the guy off the roof.

Nick Names

This guy had one leg. They called him "IHOP." They'd say, "Here comes IHOP." Has anybody called up IHOP today? Is IHOP playing hopscotch? What the fuck is this? Leave the fuckin' guy alone, he had one leg. What are you bothering the guy for? Later on, years later, they made a joke out of it. They said " Where does a guy with one leg go? The answer was IHOP. That was much later. I don't remember the guy's name.

There was this guy his name was Patsy. He owned a candy store on Jones Street between Bleecker and West 4th Streets. He was in a wheelchair. He had no legs. I feel sorry for the guy. Every time we went into the store he was in the back of the store and we used to steal the candy and run out. When he saw us he used to wheel the wheelchair right up to the front of the store. He would never catch us. By the time he rolled up to the front of the store, I was out of there. So they named him "Speedy."

Besides the nicknames every time something happened to anyone in the neighborhood they used to leave town. If someone was seriously hurt they left town. If they got caught and had a record or something like that, they'd leave town 'cause they didn't want to be questioned by the cops. Everybody used to magically disappear. They went straight to the fuckin' airports, bus terminals, and train stations. It would be all Italians tryin' to get into the wind.

Who's Better Than You!

I'll tell ya, years ago it was fun. You're talking about a reality show. You could have easily done one back then.

The Italians they're just so funny.

CHAPTER 33

THE SPANISH GUY

There is this Spanish guy in the neighborhood. Never asked him his name. He would show up at the oddest times. He is still at it.

He would stand by the curb or in the street. You know he would flip a coin and either him or you could call it, heads or tails. He'd give you 100 to 1 odds. Good odds. But I do remember how he started off. He had a few hundred dollar bills that were phony bills. So if you won, you won a hundred-dollar phony bill, and if he won he would get a real dollar.

After a while, he started using real money. He stops me in the street and he says, "Come on, come on, come on." You know when he flipped me heads or tails, he would put a hundred dollars down and he would win just like that. He pulls out the money and throws it right down on the ground. You put yours there and either he throws a coin up in the air and you call it, or you flip the coin, and he calls it. And he gives you 100 to 1. I won a couple of times, and the hundred dollars was real when I won. He won't let you quit that easy. He wants a chance to get even. He'll double up on you twice, three times, so he gets all his fuckin' money back. But if he won a few dollars then all of a sudden if he got three dollars, five dollars in his pocket he'll say, "Oh shit, I gotta go." And he wants to leave with that money, but he won't let you leave with his money.

Now all of a sudden he's doing it legitimate, he's selling jewelry. Where he gets the jewelry from I don't know. I don't ask him. But if a bracelet sells for a thousand dollars in the store, he'll sell it to you for one hundred and fifty dollars. I don't know where he gets it. Who knows if he shoplifted all this shit, or if he's stealing? But he's a real good "salesman."

He knows what he's doing.

Got my foot on the scharole!

CHAPTER 34

MY WIFE

Well, now I got a wife. I don't know if she is looking to kill me or what. I don't hear too good in my left ear 'cause a speaker blew up about ten years ago and I lost about 65% of my hearing in my left ear and about 25% in my right ear. So when I go to sleep she sleeps on one side, the 25% side. We have two televisions, one on her side of the bed and one on my side. She likes all these reality shows. I don't watch that shit. So when we switch channels it gets all fucked up. Now, she snores like she's chopping fuckin' wood. So, now I have to hear her because she's on the 25% side. Even if I turn the other way it's a problem 'cause of the enormous noise coming from her. So I put my sound up louder, louder, louder.

So she came up with an idea with headphones. I know I shouldn't have listened to her because I know she's trying to kill me. So she got me these headphones and I know that the bitch is trying to kill me because when I wake up in the middle of the night the headphones are all over my face and the chord's wrapped around my fuckin' neck. Then that's a whole other story.

And then I told her, "Honey, look I don't want to fight with you. Please, you snore and it's bad news, you're very loud. Would you mind if I bought one of those things that they show you in the drugstore. The ones you put on your nose? She said, "Buy one and put it on your dick."

She's mean. I try not to fight with her, I really do try, 'cause she's a good girl. She doesn't like to go to any of my events. She doesn't go nowhere with me. She says, "Why do I have to go? I live with you, I see you all the time. But she likes to sit home, make cookies, and bake cakes.

Now, I got a new couch that has a big dent in the cushion on one side of the couch. I said, "Would you do me a favor, switch sides every once in a while, put a microwave there on that side, do anything to get rid of the dent on that side of the fuckin' couch. You eat your fuckin' cookies." Oh please. And then she says, "You got to do exercise like I do." She eats like she's got two assholes and then at night, she's in bed lying down moving her feet like she's riding a bicycle. And I says, "What in the fuck are you doing?" She says, " I'm exercising." I said, "You exercise like that with your feet in the air. There is something wrong with you."

I don't want to fight with her. I got too many things on my

My Wife

mind. I got too many things going for me. And now the only way I don't hear her snoring is if I lay on the bed facing her. Then I have to look at her. And that's another fuckin' nightmare. Not every woman is beautiful in the middle of the night or in the morning when they wake up. It's bad enough that I have bad fuckin' dreams to begin with.

I don't want to get down on her case. You know what I mean. But you know what I told her one time. This is God's honest truth. There was this show on TV where they said you can make better relationships when people wear masks. Like a Sharon Stone mask and you make love to your partner and you think it is that other person. I just asked her one day, "Honey would you mind if I bought you a mask?" She said, "You know, you're a fucking asshole, put one on your dick." I said, "Why does everything got to go over there."

I was with my wife for a while before I married her. The reason why I got married was because all the time she kept getting sick with everything, with the ass, with the teeth, with the ears, I kept paying, kept paying, kept paying. I said I'm better off if I fuckin' marry her so I can put her on my insurance.

Ever since I married her, she hasn't had a fuckin' cold.

Nothin'!

Who's Better Than You!

CHAPTER 35

DON'T BELIEVE THAT SICK BASTARD

I was walking around with my friend Mario. We were in my neighborhood and I was talking to him on Mulberry Street, right near Spring Street.

So in the meantime, he was a Joe Pesci look-alike. I mean the same height, the same voice. He was dressed with a black pullover and everybody from both sides of the street were saying, "It's Joe Pesci, that's Joe Pesci."

As we were talking my wife's Cousin Barbara came up to me, and said, "Hello cousin Vinny, how are you doing?" I said, "I'm doing all right." Mario had his back to us. She said, "Who are you with?" And I said, "Don't you go to the movies? She said, "What the hell do I know?" I said, "It's Joe Pesci." "Joe Pesci! Oh my god!" She was hugging him and kissing him, grabbed a hold of him, and wouldn't let go. She did everything but screw him on the street.

She left and went back to the neighborhood in front of my

building on Elizabeth Street with all the people standing around and said, "I was just on Mulberry and Spring and you know that fuckin' nut Vinny was walking around with Joe Pesci."

"That wasn't Joe Pesci, that was a Joe Pesci look-alike," she was told. "That sick bastard he had me believing that was Joe Pesci." Then she said, "When I get that motherfucker…" She was calling me every name in the book. The next time I saw her she said, "You sick bastard you had me hugging and kissing this fuckin' guy in the street. You told me it was Joe Pesci. You son of a bitch."

So we got over that one.

Some time passed and the next thing you know we are at my wedding reception. Mario walks in and Cousin Barbara starts telling everyone near her about the incident with Mario and how I had tricked her.

Now before the wedding reception I told Margaret Ann I had a little surprise for her.

A little while later Robert De Niro walks in.

Nobody knew he was coming to the reception because he told me, "If anybody knows that I'm coming to the wedding I'll back out. I don't want no photographers, nobody else." So I couldn't tell anybody, not even Margaret Ann.

So anyway after De Niro walked in, the first thing Cous-

Don't Beleive That Sick Bastard

in Barbara does is come over to me and says, "What do you think you're going to fuck me over again." Then she says to Margaret Ann, "Don't mind your husband, that sick bastard he already got me once." Everyone was saying hello to Robert De Niro. It was a nice surprise to everyone.

Cousin Barbara is walking up to everybody and saying, "He isn't De Niro. Don't mind Vinny, he is a sick bastard. He's not going to fool me; he did the same thing with me, with the Joe Pesci look-alike ."

So the next thing she did, she came up to me and said, "What do you think you're going to fuck me over again. What do you think? You think I believe it is really him?" I said, "Barbara, that's fuckin' Robert De Niro!" Meanwhile, De Niro hears her and gives me a look, like what's this all about? I made a circle with my finger on the side of my head, you know the she's crazy gesture."

So finally she realized that it was the real Robert De Niro. And when she did she said to me, "I want to apologize to you."

I said, "Don't apologize to me. Go apologize to him!"

Who's Better Than You!

CHAPTER 36

THE LITTLE PERSON AND COLD STEAKS

There was this girl I met. I did not want to take her out, maybe just go out for a drink and spend some time with her. So I took her to this restaurant, and I told the waiter, "Put me in back because people recognize me and I don't want to be disturbed." I had been a regular there, so I got accommodated.

So there I was sitting in the back and this woman comes over to me and she says, "Is there any way I can get a picture with you?" I says, "Yeah, but I am eating a steak and I don't want it to get cold. Where are you sitting?" She said, "I'm over there. I said, "I'll be done in a minute, and I'll come right over to you." She goes, "Well we're ready to leave in a minute." I said, "Well you are going to have to wait, I don't want it to get cold."

So she walks away and makes a U-turn and comes right back and says, "Are you ready now?" She said, "I don't know what the big deal is." I said, "Well you are going to have to wait,

Who's Better Than You!

I don't want my steak to get cold." She said, "I don't think you know who the hell you are!" I said, "I know who I am, who the hell do you think you are!" I says," You are being a little rude. Now, I don't want to take a picture with you. Do me a favor, why don't you get the hell out of here." She said, "Why don't you say that to my husband." I said, "Go get your husband."

She goes to get her husband and they come back and she says, "Here, say that to my husband." I turned around and the guy was a midget. He was no bigger than a pair of boots. He says, "Hey man, you bad-mouthed my wife." I said, "Come on man, I don't want no problems, your wife was being very rude. I don't want to take a picture with her, and I don't want no problems." He said, "You bad-mouth my wife like that again, and I will kick your ass." I said, "I don't think you could reach my ass." He was looking on the table for something to hurt me or to hit me with. I don't know whether it was a fork or spoon or something else.

So finally the owner comes over and they got him out of there. The girl I was sitting with said, "I am going to go; I am afraid of you." I told her, "Look how rude the lady was."

So she sat back down, and I had to pay for two cold steaks.

CHAPTER 37

MAUSOLEUM SHOPPING TRIP

You got to know that a lot of times some people think my cousin, me, and my mother, maybe it was a dysfunctional family. Well, let's put it this way, with my cousin I could say alright yeah, with me that's another story, and with my mother, she's another story. Now I no longer have my mother and father.

Just before my mother and father passed away, my father says to me, " Please Vinny do me a big a favor. Go with Mama to the cemetery and buy the mausoleum for me, for your cousin, and for Mama. But don't put your cousin next to me. Put Mama in the middle, put Angelo over there, and me on the other end. I said, "Okay."

We go there, Mom, me and my cousin. This sales guy is showing us all these mausoleums.

So the guy says, "I got those three up there." My mother says, "No, no. I no like it over there. I get a dizzy. It's a too high." I said, Ma how the fuck you're gonna get dizzy? If you're dead you're up there, you're not gonna get dizzy. The sales guy is looking at me. I said to the guy, "Why the fuck are you looking at me for, she's the one who said it."

He had the ones down there at the bottom which he suggested. It turned out the ones you could look at and touch standing straight up, were a little more money. The sales guy points to the lowest level and says, "Would you like these three?" "No, no. Some a times the dust, it get on the floor. No, no I no like it." I said, "Ma you're giving the guy a hard time." And my cousin would say stupid things.

Finally, we came to one area. The sales guy says, "I got two of youse together in one area over there and this one at the end." My cousin said, "Well who is over there that would be next to me? The guy said, "A professor." My cousin says, "I'll take that one. At least I'll have someone to talk to."

Once again the guy is looking at me. I told the guy straight out, "Why the fuck you lookin' at me for, he's the one who said it."

So he writes it up for the three mausoleums. He goes to me, "Do you want one in here also sir?" I said, "Me? I don't even want one in this fuckin' building. I want another cemetery. I don't want one here!"

CHAPTER 38

LA BELLA FERRARA

In Little Italy I like to hang out at La Bella Ferrara's because there are these two brothers, Nick and Frank who own the place. They're friends of mine. I've known them for years since 1970 since they have the store, that's 42 years. There is

left to right: Frank and Nick

the bakery and the café next to each other. They are great guys the two of them. I love the two of them. I know their whole families, their wives their kids.

So there is just one waitress I got to get her fired.

I like the atmosphere of the place. Frank puts on some music occasionally and sings songs in Italian. The cappuccino is great. There is pastry which I don't eat much, no more. But you can get the best cannoli's, sfogliatelle, cakes, etc. The pastry is all made on the premises, so it's always fresh. I like the idea of being able to sit outside where you can hang out.

When I sit down people they recognize me. All the beautiful people you see all day long. Beautiful women, tourists from all around and they recognize ya and want to take pictures with ya. As much as they enjoy taking pictures with me, I enjoy taking pictures with them. I get in conversations with them, tell them my stories and they all want my email and want to email me. I do email them back.

I just love everyone there, except for that one waitress.

I'll just want to go back there and see what I can do to get her fired.

Two days after I met these people at La Bella Ferrara they called me and wanted me to come to their daughter's wedding on a Sunday. This happens a lot. They were so excited to meet me. Had to say no. Previous commitment.

Vinny is sitting outside La Bella Ferrara on January 13th, 2013, the final day of La Bella Ferrara café. Vinny says "Here we are sitting outside La Bella Ferrara the café, not the bakery. It's been here since 1970 and 43 years later the landlord raised his rent from $8,000 to $16,000.

The guy who owns this building I'd like to take him for a walk actually, and by the time he comes back they'll be paying $4,000 for rent."

Who's Better Than You!

CHAPTER 39

JOKES

I

There was this patrol car that was sitting on the side of the road. There was a guy driving a car and he sees this patrol car as he is going past it. He stepped on the gas. He took off. So the patrol car chases him through two towns. And the cop car caught up to him and he goes "You know what? You're really pissing me off man. I was just trying to get off duty and you seen me and as soon as you seen me, you took off. You give me one good reason why you did this and maybe I'll go easy on you." The driver said, "Last year my wife took off with a State Trooper. When I seen you were chasing me I thought you were bringing her back."

II

This guy he's working in a machine shop and turned around and said hello to his friend and the machine came down and chopped off his arm. He took his arm. he put it in the bag and he held his arm up to stop the blood from draining out and went to the hospital. He is Italian and he goes, "Doctor, Doctor please my arm it's a come off. I got it in the bag with the ice. Please you put it back on for me." "Yeah I can do that but it's going to cost you $10,000." "No, no, no please, I'm the only one that a work, and my wife she's a sick, I have the same shop for 22 years so how about I pay you so much every week." The doctor says "I take cash. No credit, no credit cards I just take cash." "Please a doctor I got a work. Please I pay you something." The doctor says, "No I can't do it."

He left the hospital and he was crying and he went past this shoe store. Jimmy the shoemaker also Italian came out and he said, "Giuseppe what's a matter. How come you are a crying?" "I lose a my arm. I got the thing in a bag with the ice. I go to the hospital and that son of a bitch doctor he no want to fix it. $10,000 I don't have the money." Jmmy says, "It's all right Giuseppe relax I fix for you." "How the hell are you going to fix? You a shoemaker." "Don't worry I gonna fix for you." "How much?" "Give me five dollars." "Five dollars?" He fixes it. "Look at this you did a good job; I don't believe this shit. I'm gonna run to the hospital. I'm gonna show that son of a bitch doctor what you did for five dollars."

He goes back to the hospital and finds the Doctor. The Doctor says, "I don't believe it, he did a good job." Giuseppe says,

Jokes

"Come over here Doctor. My friend he fix my arm for five dollars, you know what I got to say to you? He puts his hand across his fixed arm to signal "Up Yours," and the arm goes flying.

III

True Story. I went to an Italian restaurant not too long ago. It was my friend's grandfather's birthday. So he said, "Vinny could you at least come and say hello to him." I said, "Sure. "His grandfather was celebrating his 99th birthday. So I was there and I went over to the grandfather and lifted a drink in my hand and I said, "Salud, Chin Don which means good health for a hundred years. And he turned around and said, "Fuck you, what, are you only giving me one year?"

That guy was funny.

Who's Better Than You!

CHAPTER 40

MARRIAGE

My first wife came from a very rich family. I first met her on the beach, Miami Beach. I used to hang out on 48th Street right next to the parking lot of the Eden Roc. Everybody used to hang out back then. I was hanging out with all the girls and the guys there and that's how I got to meet her. She used to be there all the time and I like had a crush on her. So finally I get to meet her, and you know, date her a little bit. But the dates were always on the beach or being alone down there away from anybody else. We would be lying down there on a blanket, meeting sometimes for lunch. But she would never let me take her home. I figured she probably didn't want me to know that she came from a family with money. She probably wanted to see if I was going to like her for who she was.

So every day she wouldn't let me bring her home. I had a motor scooter. She would take the bus home. She said to me, "I would rather go by bus." I wanted to see where the fuck she lived. So one day I had my friend, he had a car, so I said to my friend, "Do me a favor, when she gets on the bus I'm going to go around the corner and hop into your car. I want you to follow the bus, I want to see where she lives." She lived in an area called Pine Tree Drive. So when she got off the bus she walked down this long street and made a left. It was right where these expensive homes were. So after she made the left we went up the block and she disappeared. So there were these two pillars in front of her house. My friend ran up to the pillars and came back and asked me what her last name was. I told him the name. He goes, "That's where she lives." I said, "How do you know that?" He said, "In the pillars, there was a light and it spelled out the name." I came to find out that the mother was married five times. Forget about it, that's another case.

She finally said, "My mother and father want to meet you." So I met her mother. She was a woman who for her age was sharp. She was like in her 40s or 50s at that time. She had some mouthpiece, this woman. She said, "Where are you living? I said, "Well I am staying down in this hotel."

Actually, I couldn't afford the rent anymore in the apartment I had, so now I was living on the beach. I used to bury my suitcase in the sand with all my clothes. There was a shower on the beach and the water would come out nice and warm. Then I would go into a restaurant bathroom, plug in my shaver and

Marriage

clean up. I robbed tips off the tables. That's how I was making a living. So she said, "We have an extra bedroom here so you could stay with us." So I moved into the house.

I ended up being married to her for five years and then we moved back to New York. My father was okay with my wife, but to my mother, she was no good. It didn't work out. So much of it was me and not her. I started cheating on her and all that stuff.

They say what goes around comes around and I left her. Years later I met this other girl. I was thirty-three years old and she was eighteen and I married her. What I did to my first wife, boy did I get it back from this one. Talk about catchin' a beating, boy did she give it to me. That was the second wife. Then I was single for the longest time and it just kept getting worse, didn't get any better. You know they say it gets worse before it gets better.

I was married for a third time. My third marriage was with a good girl and all that. I wound up with a beautiful son. Margaret Ann was recently divorced with two kids Benjamin and Anthony. She knew I had a bad habit. She was neglecting what she had to do with her money and giving it to me. Her kids were doing without new shoes and sneakers at that point in time. At one point she said to me, "Honey I love you but, do you think maybe you could slow down a little bit because the kids have holes in their shoes and we are not eating the same way we used to eat. Can you do that for just a little while?" I felt like such a little man when she told me that. From that point on I just stopped and I never used it again. We got out of the hole and stood out of the hole from that day on. I never forgot what she did for me.

My choice of drugs was cocaine. Then I started freebasing and then it got worse. When I stopped I had $300 of cocaine left. I said I am not going to flush it down the toilet, I'm gonna go out, sell it, and get the money back. That's what I did. Never used it since and I started hustling back then to get a hold of some money. Those holes in the shoes became new shoes and the food on the table became good food. We were eating steaks again.

When I was back to where I was before, not doing the drugs, a friend of mine came around one night, said hello to me from his car and I hopped in with him. He said, "Vinnie do you want to do a line? Now I'm a coke connoisseur I can just tell you by just looking at it, I don't have to taste it to know whether it is good. I looked at it and I said, "No, no." I realized that when you do cocaine you never get enough of it. You do it and you want another hit, and another hit, and so on.

I used to kid around with Margaret Ann a little bit and still do today. "Hey, give me a kiss." "What are you gonna get me?" I said, What do you want?" She said, "How about those pajamas at Victoria's Secret." "No problem, how much are they? She said, "$59." I said, "Sleep naked."

Her mother Millie is the best woman on this earth. She is not only my friend, she's like a sister to me. She's my best friend, she is like everything to me, she is such a sweetheart. At one point she said, "We love him, but his elevator does not go all the way up." I tease her sometimes and I tell everybody, "That's my girlfriend." She says, "Don't mind him, he needs a doctor."

After all the drugs that I've used and after all that I've been through, anybody else would have had their nose donated to science. Their nose would have fell off their face and they would have been dead. I never went to a drug rehabilitation center. I just woke up one morning and I said, "That's it." And I never used again.

Then Margaret Ann got pregnant and when she went for the sonogram they told us it was a boy. I always wanted a little boy. I finally got it. And when little Vinny came out, it had to be Vinny Vella Jr.

We won't go any further than that.

Who's Better Than You!

Vinny Vella, Jr.

CHAPTER 41

NO ONE IS GOING TO SCREW ME

I go out to these different restaurants and bars to promote groups and businesses. I get a percentage of the take and usually my drinks and food are most often taken care of by the management of the place.

So this one night I went to this nightclub and checked in with the manager and then went about my business promoting the group that invited me to appear. I did my usual thing of talking to people, answering their questions, signing autographs, and taking pictures.

At the end of the night, the manager wants to stick me with the tab for my drinks. It was $7. I had already gotten paid by the group that got me to come in, so that was water under the bridge. The manager was no good. He was a new guy that they put in charge and the guy was playing hardball and he didn't know he was playing hardball with the wrong guy. I paid the tab.

Who's Better Than You!

So I had to screw him on the way out 'cause he was trying to fuck me. So at the bar were these six girls who said to me, "Aren't you the guy in *Casino*, the actor." I said, "Yeah" and I started talking with them. There were these two guys sitting alongside of them, trying to talk to them and make them. So I went up to the bartender and I pulled out money like I was going to pay for them and I said, "Hey bartender do me a favor, buy these girls a drink and you know what, give these two guys a drink too. Buy all of them a drink on me."

So I had to use a little psychology. I went to the end of the bar and asked the bartender for a glass of water and said, "Run a tab on those drinks." After the drinks were poured I began to walk out and said goodbye to the people. The bartender said, "Excuse me you owe me for these drinks over here." I said, "Go give it to that prick manager in the kitchen or wherever he's hiding, tell him to put it in on my tab and tell him to go fuck himself."

He screwed me but I got him back 10 times what he got from me.

CHAPTER 42

THE MOVIE "DIRECTOR"

I had this one guy. I did a movie. The guy said he was a "Director" even though he never directed anything before. He wanted to be an actor too and he's not even in SAG, the union.

He called me on the phone to do this movie. "Well," he said, "It's a low budget." I said, "I can't do it for nothing." He said, "What do you want?" I said, "I got to get at least $1,500 for the day." He said, "Vinny I don't have that kind of money." So I said, "How much you want to pay me?" He says,"$500." I said, "No way, the least I'll do it for is $1,000. That would be cash. Cash when I get there, not when I'm done. When we start to work is when I want the money."

So I get there a few days later. I said, "Did you forget you're supposed to give me the money." "Oh yeah.." He gives me $600. I said, "Where is the other $400?" He says, "The guy went to the bank, he'll be back in a little while. Please just give him enough time to go to the bank because I switched banks so there is a little problem. I got to wait till the money clears this afternoon."

The script lines that I had up to that time, were little paragraphs, and all of a sudden he says, "I want to change this. I want you to do this now." Now they weren't paragraphs anymore, it was like the whole sheet was like a monologue and I said, "Whoa! Whoa! Whoa! Where did you come up with this?" He said, "Let's take a break. Just read it for about 10 minutes and then we'll do this." "Read it for 10 minutes! I said, "You put a whole monologue over here. There's hundreds of words over here. There's no way I can do that. It took me a week to memorize these freaking few lines over there. You want me to do this whole monologue?" So we took a break.

We came back from the break and he said, "Did you memorize this?" I said, "No I didn't." He says, "Okay you know what we'll do." I said, "No." "He said, "We'll do one line at a time." So we did the one line and he says, "Okay cut, and now let's do the second line." Then he says, "Cut and the third line." Then he said, "Cut." I said, "Do you know what you're doing? I've never done anything like this before. One line cut, one line cut, one line cut. How are you going to do this?"

So it wasn't really working out. Then he says, "Even my line producer says you're the worst actor we've ever worked with before." I said, "Whoa! Whoa! Whoa! Let's get something straight over here. First of all, you never directed any-

The Movie "Director"

thing before in your life except maybe for traffic. You don't even act. When you put yourself in the fucking shot you don't even know what you're doing. You want to talk about me, I'm the worst actor you've ever worked with. I've been in more movies longer than your line producer's age. What the fuck are you kidding me, or what." I said, "Where's my fucking money!" He said, "The money is coming."

At the end of the day I said, "Where's my money?" He says, "I'll have to pay you tomorrow, we had a little problem."

So I call him up the next day and he says, "I'll come down. I'll meet you and I'll give you the money." So we got to La Bella Ferrara's on a summer day. We're sitting down. He says, "Before I give you the money you got to sign this thing over here." So I sign it. He pulls the paper back towards him and says, "Did you really think I was going to pay you?" I said, "What!" I pulled the paper back and I ripped it up. He said, "I don't really need that." It was in a hundred little pieces. So I take his camera and he says, "Whoa! Whoa! Whoa!" I said, "You got my fucking money?" I busted the camera right there on the spot.

Now I had to get up because I don't want Frank and his customers distracted and all that. He said, "That was 600 fucking dollars that I paid for that fucking camera." So I said, "You know what you do. With the $400 that you still owe me, you put another $200 and you buy yourself a new camera!" He said, "I want money for what you just did! You wrecked my camera!" I said, "Listen to me. Let me tell you something, as far as I'm concerned you still owe me $400." "How about my camera? he said. "I don't give a fuck about your camera! You fuck me, I'm going to fuck you! I want my $400. If you don't give me $400 I'm going to put you all over the internet and you won't be able to do a fucking student film when I get done with you. I'll bad mouth you like you've never been bad-mouthed before and you want to know something, you better never come to this fucking neighborhood no more. If you ever come to this neighborhood, wherever they see you that's where they're going to find you. Don't come around here. You know why? Because I'm one sick Italian and sometimes I don't fucking think. You know why? 'Cause I'm fucking stupid. You know what, don't come around here no more." So that was that.

So meanwhile Frank came over and says, "What do you do? What you break? You break a the camera? I said don't worry Frank, he's on his way home. He dropped the camera." "I didn't drop the camera, he broke it!" he said. I said, "Whatever. It's broke, go home, no big thing."

I used to always tell my friends that if anybody wants you to do a movie, always check with me because I know all these

The Movie "Director"

people in the industry. I know if they are bullshiting or not. So this guy from Canarsie his name is Steve and he gives me a call and says, "This guy's going to pay me $100 to be in his movie." It was the same guy the "Director". "Steve," I said, "You do not want to do it because you will wind up getting fucked by this guy." I said, "I'll give you $50, don't do it and you'll make $50 for doing nothing. Just one condition, I want you to go back to him and say I can't do it because Vinny is a friend of mine and he told me I shouldn't do it. The reason why? He said, You were a no good, motherfucker."

The guy is still out there doing movies.

I'm too nice a guy, so I won't mention his name.

Who's Better Than You!

San Gennaro Festival

CHAPTER 43

SAN GENNARO FESTIVAL ICE PICK ACCIDENT

I'll never forget it was another incident a few years ago where I don't remember what happened but, somebody joined the San Gennaro Festival and put an ice pick in a guy's back.

The guy joined the crowd walked right behind him and stuck a fucking ice pick in his back. The guy collapsed.

So the guy just before that like an hour before, he was sitting down with me. I know the guy, but he was a fucking rat and I don't want to be around rats. So somehow the word got out that he was sitting with me.

The cops came over to me and said, "This guy got stabbed in the back"… badaboop, badabap. "They said he was sitting with you."

"Sitting with me doesn't mean I stabbed him."

So this guy's a rat and I don't deal with rats. But I happened to be nice to him because I didn't want to embarrass him. So he sat with me for a few minutes. He didn't even order nothing and then he left.

They said, "What do you think happened?"

I said, "I don't know, as far as I'm concerned the guy maybe accidentally stabbed himself in the back a couple of times, and then he collapsed."

One of the cops said," What?"

I said, "What the fuck do I know, you're asking me."

The cop said, "How could a guy accidentally stab himself in the back?"

"What are you asking me questions for? I don't know what you're talking about. You don't know what I'm talking about. What the fuck are we talking about."

The cop says, "There's something wrong with you."

CHAPTER 44

HAVE YOU EVER HAD A WOMAN LIKE ME BEFORE?

The Duprees manager set them up to perform at a place called the Dessert Bar in the Sands Hotel which is no longer there.

The Duprees gave me an introduction and I went up on stage. I talked for a few minutes and then I brought on the Duprees. After that, I went back up there again, thanked the people and The Duprees, blah blah blah. I talked for another minute or two. Then I said, We're going to be out in the lobby signing autographs."

When I was in the lobby signing autographs I had this old woman, she came behind me and grabbed my ass. I says, "Sweetheart you can't do that." I said, "My wife is around here, she's Puerto Rican and if she sees you doing that, you know you're going to get me in a lot of trouble."

She goes, "Okay have you ever had a woman like me before?" I said, "No I haven't." She goes, "How old do you think

Who's Better Than You!

I am?" Now I wanted her to feel good. I said, "I don't know like 63, 64." She says, "I'm 70 and nobody believes it."

That old bitch wasn't 70, she was about 90, and when she left she gave me another pat on my ass and walked out.

CHAPTER 45

GOOD THING I'M VINNY VELLA

So now I had to go for the results of what my problem was with my right knee. So they took X-rays and all that.

The doctor came in, blah, blah, blah, blah, blah. He says, "You're pretty lucky we thought maybe it might have been water, swelling, or maybe a kneecap." But, then he said, "You have a little arthritis in your right knee." So I says, "That arthritis doesn't move anywhere, does it? It's not going to affect anything else down there is it?"

That doctor started laughing. So then another doctor came by and he says to me, "I like your work." So the other doctor says, "What do you mean you like his work? How'd you know who he is?" "Oh my God, that's right, he's the guy from *Casino*."

I'm taking pictures, taking pictures, taking pictures. I said "Doc, not for nothing, but I got arthritis, you sure I'm not going to have any problems like from the waist down? You know I got enough problems as it is." "You may have problems from the waist up, but not from the waist down that's all you have."

And then I'm taking pictures with all the nurses and all.

There are patients out there that are fuckin' bleeding that need to be seen and the visiting room is packed with people. I'm feeling bad you know, 'cause these people are there who need to see the doctor. You know I'm over there taking pictures and nobody's working. Everyone wants to take pictures with me and I felt bad, I felt bad about it you know.

I told the doctor of my concern, he said, "Don't worry about them, they're not going nowhere." That was his attitude.

Good thing I'm Vinny Vella, I'll tell you that much.

CHAPTER 46

I WOULD HAVE BEEN BETTER OFF TRAVELING TO JAMAICA, QUEENS

So we decide to take a trip to Jamaica. The vacation was okay.

On the way home the Security Officer in the airport saw this chain I had on. It was an 18-karat gold chain that had been given to me and a few other people at some function. The chain had a gun on it with a diamond bullet.

So I see this Security Officer come over to me and he was clearly eyeing the chain. I thought, here we go an international incident is about to take place.

He says to me, "You have to take off that chain and put it in your luggage." What do you mean I got to put it away in my luggage? My luggage already went past, through the conveyor belt. He says, "You have to give it to me." "No, you ain't taking my chain." "But there is a gun on it." "Well, it doesn't shoot real bullets." "Yeah, but it is a gun! You're not allowed to wear it because it represents something bad." This went on for a while.

Margaret Ann saw what was happening and she knew from the tone of my voice where this conversation was going to go. She went over to a Supervisor and said, "That Security Guard wants my husband's necklace and it's not going to happen. I can put it in my purse." The Supervisor came over, checked out the situation and told the Security Guard to let Margaret Ann put the chain in her purse.

So that seemed to resolve the situation except that the Security Guard said, "I'm going to check on you until you get on the plane. If you are wearing it at any time I'm going to take it away from you." I said "Fuck you! You ain't going to take nothing from me! You're not taking this. You're going to have to kill me first."

Our flight was delayed and he kept checking up on me.

I never went to Jamaica again because they were all a bunch of crooks.

I still got the chain.

I Would Have Been Better Off Travelling to Jamaica Queens

"You ain't going to take nothing from me!
You're not taking this.
You're going to have to kill me first."

Who's Better Than You!

CHAPTER 47

I NEED A NEW TRAVEL AGENT

So Margaret Ann decided one Valentine's Day she was going to surprise me with a trip to Florida.

I swear to you it was the last time she ever bought us airplane tickets, 'cause I was never going to let this one happen to me ever again.

Somewhere she read that there was a Valentine's Day special where you could buy an adult airplane ticket and you would get a child's airplane ticket for free. She told me they were really, really, inexpensive. She goes and buys two adult tickets so we could take Anthony and Vincent, who were young at the time, along with us. The kids were out of school because of the winter break.

Now, I was exhausted because the night before I was doing a movie and the shoot ran late. She schedules us to leave at 10:00 a.m. so we would get to Florida around 1:00 p.m. When she booked the flight I'm not sure what clock she was looking at or whether she was wearing her glasses. It turns out the flight she booked stopped in every other state going down the East Coast. By the time we reached Florida it was 1:00 a.m. the next day! We spent as much time on the ground as we did in the air with all those fuckin' stops.

It seemed like every half hour we'd land, be delayed, let people off, let new people on, refuel the plane, and all that shit. So I'm trying to sleep and every time I thought I was in a deep sleep I woke up to the announcements that we were landing, buckle your seat belts, what number conveyor belt to pick up your luggage on, what the next destination was, how long the flight was, did I want a snack, did I want a drink, blah, blah, blah. I said to Margaret Ann, "Tell the stewardess to leave me the fuck alone. I got to get some sleep." Every time the plane stopped I woke up thinking I was in Florida.

The whole trip took 13 fuckin' hours!

I knew I had to get a new travel agent.

CHAPTER 48

MARGARET ANN SHARES A STORY

So one day Vinny got hired by a Japanese company.

They were filming people in New York for a Japanese television show which would air in Japan. They wanted to see how much money women would accept to be filmed lifting their shirts and shaking their breasts.

So one night he called me up and he asked me what I was doing. I said, "Nothing, I'm putting the baby to sleep." He says, "You want to make $200?" I said, "$200 doing what?" He said, "You have to lift your shirt up and shake your breasts." So I'm like, "Are you fucking kidding me!" I said, "Do me a favor, leave me alone," and I hang up the phone. So a little while later after maybe about 40 minutes, he calls me up and says, "Do you want to make $300?" I'm like, "Leave me alone, I'm trying to put the baby to sleep. What's wrong with you?" He said, "But you could make $300." I said, "I don't care. Go fuck yourself," and I hang up.

Five minutes later my cousin Barbara calls me up and she says, "What the fuck is wrong with your husband?" I'm like, "What, what is it?" Barbara said, "He called me up and he wanted to know if I wanted to make $300. I got to shake my breasts. Is he kidding me?" I said, "Barbara just hang up on him the next time he calls you."

Couple of minutes later my sister calls me. She tells me the same thing. "What the fuck is wrong with Vinny? Is he kidding me, it's 8:00 at night. He wants me to go to a location and shake my breasts for $300." I'm like, "Oh don't mind him. When he calls you again just hang up."

No more than 20 minutes passed and he calls me up and says, "Do you want to make $500?" I'm like, "Are you fucking kidding me? I said, "Whose dick do I have to suck for $500?" He says, "No I'm serious, this is for a Japanese television show. They just want to see how much money it would take for a woman to show her breasts and shake them." I said, "Vinny go fuck yourself." and I hang up the phone.

Two days later I want to go Christmas shopping. I called Vinny up while he was working in the Star Truckers vehicle and I said, "Do me a favor could you call up the Japanese guy? Tell him for $500 I'll get naked! I need Christmas money." My husband told me to go fuck myself and he hung up on me politely, or maybe not so politely.

I guess they didn't get too many takers at $200 and $300, but when they upped it to $500, I guess that's when they got many takers. But not me!

CHAPTER 49

KING TUT'S RING

Now with King Tut's ring let me be perfectly clear. I had absolutely nothing to do with the disappearance of the ring from the museum, but somehow, you know, it wound up in my hands. It's an unbelievable story.

I was involved with this jewelry store. Somebody had come into the store and sold the ring to the owner of the store. There was a little money involved that the jewelry store owner was going to give me for returning the ring to the museum. So when it came time to return the ring, I was acting as his representative.

So I called up the museum and I said, "I'd like to speak to head of security of the museum. They said, "What is this in reference to?" I said, "This is in reference to King Tut's jewelry." "Who may I ask is calling." "Aw, just call me Joe." "Joe what?" "Joe's good enough." They said, "Hold on." I said, "Just get head security near the phone. I'll call back in about 10-15 minutes." So I did call back. They said, "Who's calling?" I said, "Joe." "What's this in reference to?" I said, "Listen, I'm not going to keep going through this. This is in reference to King Tut's jewelry." "Now is the head of the museum security there?" "Could you hold on just one moment?" I said, "Listen to me I'm not going to keep holding on. I'll call you back again and if he's not there forget about it, but you're missing a piece of jewelry that's from King Tut and you're not going to get it back unless the head security is there and I want to talk to this guy."

So I called back. I said, "All right this is Joe I want to talk to head security." This guy says, "I'm head security." I asked him, "What's your name?" He said, "Robert L." I'll never forget. I said, "You happen to be missing a piece of jewelry and I'm a reputable businessman in the neighborhood. What I want to do is, I want to bring it back to you." "Oh that's very nice of you and how did you get a hold of it?" "It doesn't matter, but you know I'd like to get back the money I paid for it." "How much did you pay for it?" I said, "$10,000." He said, "$10,000, okay, okay, just bring it back." "Where do you want..." I said, "Look I've been on the phone long enough. I'll call you back." I didn't want them to trace the call.

So I called him back and he said, "Where would you want to meet?" I said, "First before we meet let's get something clear. When I meet with you I want a note stating that I won't

I Would Have Been Better Off Travelling to Jamaica Queens

be responsible for the theft of the ring and upon returning it, I get a sum of $10,000. In addition, I want you to sign the note in front of me. When I meet you I'm not going to have the ring on me and if I'm arrested or anything else happens, you'll never see the ring again." Okay, where do you want to meet? "85th Street near the museum on 5th Avenue." "Okay fine." "What are you going to be wearing," "He said, "I'll have a plaid jacket, or something like that, like plaid pants. Just come over to me and say Cleopatra and I'll give you the note." I said, "Okay fine."

So when I got there, there were like two, three people with fucking plaid pants, plaid jackets. So I said oh shit. So I went to the first guy. With my luck, it ended up being the third guy. I went over to one guy, and said, "Cleopatra." He said, "Excuse me?" I said, "How often do the buses come down 5th Avenue?" So I figured it wasn't him. I went over to the second guy. I said, "Cleopatra." He said, "Excuse me?" I said, "What time is it?" I said to myself, what the fuck man. So I went over to the third guy and said, "Cleopatra." He said "What?" I said, "Cleopatra." He said, "Oh yeah." So he goes in his back pocket. I said, "How come you put the note in your back pocket? Can't you be a normal guy and put it in your front pocket? You made me feel like you were reaching for something over here." I looked at the note and I said, "I told you I wanted you to sign that note in front of me. There is already a signature on the note. Now you know what. I am going to turn the note over and have you sign it again. If that signature isn't the same as this one, we are not doing any business." He signed it again. The signatures matched up. I said, "Okay, what do you want me to do now?" Do whatever you want. Go in the park, go play on the swings. Do something. I'll get in touch with you. Don't worry about it we'll take it from there."

So we made a meeting place to exchange the ring. It was 72nd Street between 5th and Madison in an art gallery. He says, "When you ring the bell just tell them your name is Joe and they'll let you in. I'll be in there waiting for you." I said, "Okay fine."

I go over there and have the ring in my pocket and now remember, I didn't steal this ring. I ring the bell and a woman answers. She says, "May I help you." I said, "My name is Joe." She says, "Go inside" and she looked a little frightened. I go inside and she ran. I figured she knew who I was or she was expecting me.

So I walked into this gallery, then into another room and it was one big, huge room, no furniture nothing. There was a fireplace and one big picture hanging up above the fireplace and the fireplace had like a little ledge on it. So when I walked in he goes "Did you bring the ring?" I said, "Yeah." I says,

King Tut's Ring

"You got the money?" He says, "Yeah." So I take the ring out of my pocket and he goes, "Is that how you brought it here?" I said, "What do you want me to do carry it in on a fucking pillow?" So he gives me the money and he is shelling it out and he's looking in a book about the ring, checking it out, and he keeps walking around me. I said, "Would you stay still. You're getting me nervous." He said, "I'm just excited that I got this ring back. I have to make sure this is the right ring" and he kept walking all around. He said, "But do me a favor count the money." I took the money fanning it near my ear and I said, "Don't worry the weight is good." He says, "No, I want you to count the money 'cause I don't want any more problems with you. I never want to see you again." I said, "Ah, don't worry about it."

So he kept distracting me walking back and forth. So at one point, I started counting the money. All of a sudden there was movement to my left. I didn't watch him for one moment 'cause I was distracted by the money, so he ran behind me. He was about 7-8 feet away and from his ankle he pulled up a gun, a 9 millimeter, He pointed it right at me.

There was a camera up on the wall facing that fireplace and that picture. That's where I was standing and I had the money already in my jacket. He yelled, "Give me that money." Now, if I would have reached inside my jacket to take out the money he could have said, I thought he was pulling out a gun to shoot me. It turns out that later on, I found out that he lost his job and the only way he could get his job back is if he said, I got the son of a bitch that stole the ring, here he is. But if he says, a good Samaritan just came in and returned the ring, that's not going to work for him. So when I looked at the camera I said, "Okay, no, no, no, no." I said, "Please, the money is in my jacket, you take it. He said, "Take that money out! I'm going to shoot you, you guinea bastard! I said, "You're getting me nervous. You're going to make me start fartin' if you keep pointing that gun at me. Please, get it out of my face. You can have the ring and the money, just don't shoot me."

He told me to take out the note. Then he took it from me, ripped it up and put it in his pocket. And now I've got nothin'. He shouted, "Come out now!" and another guy came in. They were like punching me and kicking me while I was on the floor and I was going with the kicks and the punches. "Ooh, ah, argh!"" I was making believe like they were hurting me. They kept asking me, "Who's involved with you on this?" I said, "Ziad S." Ziad S. was from the Middle East and had a real foreign-sounding last name. "What? What kind of fucking name is that?" And they kept hitting me. He said, "I'm going to ask you again what's the guy's name.?" I said, Ziad S." They went at it again. I said, "What do you want me to say?"

King Tut's Ring

So I said, "Okay, Joe Salami that's the guy's name."

And now the guy that was involved with me his name was Ziad S. and he was the owner from the jewelry store. He was waiting on the corner for me. He had on a long camel trench coat and he was waiting for me to come out. And then all of a sudden after they beat the hell out of me and all that, Robert L. said, "All right let them in." So all these cops and FBI men came in. I was already cuffed and all that. Meanwhile Robert L., he could have been no more than 5'5 or 5'6. He looked at me and said, "I should have killed you when I had the chance, you guinea bastard!" Then this one FBI guy who must have been about 6 ft 6, he told him, "Listen, let's cut that guinea shit. I happen to be Italian. I said, "That little prick has been calling me a guinea bastard for the last half hour." So the FBI guy says, "Looks like you got a little trouble over here." He says, "Whatever made you do it?" I said, "Do what? All I was doing was giving back the ring that the guy from the jewelry store…" He cut me off and said, "What jewelry store?" I said, "His name is Ziad S. Actually, someone came into his store and sold him the ring. He's on the corner waiting for me." They went out and got Ziad S.

Meanwhile, I got arrested.

So now I'm going out of the art gallery at 72nd Street between 5th and Madison. It was all blocked off, cops with

Who's Better Than You!

rifles behind cars and FBI guys surrounding the place. I said, Oh shit. So I went down to FBI headquarters and the District Attorney at that time came to see me.

But first, they sat me down in this dark room with a one-way mirror just like they show you on TV with a spotlight on me. They sit me down and want to know how this all started. All these FBI guys were around and they had me on camera. I told them all what happened. How I went into the room, asked the guy about putting the ring on a pillow, the guy putting a gun in my face, how he asked me who was involved, and how I said, Ziad S. Then how every time I said Ziad S. it was like Abbott and Costello's Niagara Falls routine, and the guys kept hitting me. I could tell these FBI guys are laughing even though they got their hands on their faces. I said, "You guys are smiling. That's really what the guy was doing. He asked me three times and every time I said Ziad S., they kept hitting me. The guy that was hitting me said, "I'm going to ask you one more time" and I said, "I'm not going to say it, because every time I mention the guy's name you keep hitting me." So I told them the whole thing I said, "Ziad S., he's the one from the jewelry store blah blah blah blah blah blah."

So now this is the funny part. The District Attorney came in and he said, "I'd like to speak to you. How are you?" I says, "I've seen you for a long time on TV." He wanted me to explain the whole thing to him. So after I finished and it was over he said, "You know what, I believe you. I'm going to see what I can do in the morning and get you out on your own recognizance." I said, "Oh great."

So the morning came and I got out.

So then I have a date to come back to court. They called me up after about a week and said, "Rather than you come in on the date that was set up, we want to bring this right to the Grand Jury. So we are going to move that trial date up just a few days. So would you come in?" I said, "Sure fine."

I go to the Grand Jury and who is there was the District Attorney and also the museum attorney and the head security from the museum. So when I get there, I am sitting down and they start asking me questions. Every time they kept asking me questions Robert L. and the museum attorney kept interrupting. There were three judges so I didn't know who to talk to, so I said, "Your Honor, may I say something? This one judge said, "Okay. "Every time you ask me a question they keep jumping up and interrupting my conversation with you. I'm not telling you how to run your courtroom. Is there any way you could ask them the questions first regardless of whether they are right or wrong? I ain't going to say a word and I won't interrupt them and then when it's time for me to talk I'd like that same cooperation so they don't interrupt."

The judge nodded his head.

But I'll never forget the three judges that were sitting up there, the jury sitting over there and I'm sitting down here at the bottom of the Grand Jury. I had been talking about the note earlier telling them that Robert L. had ripped up the note he had given me. Robert L. interrupted and said, "We don't give notes to criminals, plus I want you to hear what he actually said."

So all of those conversations that I had with him on the phone, he had recorded them and then he went and edited every conversation. And when he said originally "I'll come with the $10,000, I hope you have the ring" and when I said, "I don't want to be responsible for this after the ring is returned, those parts of the conversation were not on the recording he played. None of that was in there. So after they listened to tape after tape after tape there was no mention of the note and the other stuff.

Now when it came time for me to talk, one of the judges looked at me and says, "What do you have to say about that Mr. Vella?" I said, "Okay Your Honor if I may. Everything they presented on those tapes were all edited and there was no note talked about on his recording. Now I'm going to ask the people in the jury. If I was sitting where you people are sitting looking at Vinny Vella, you know what, he's guilty, I'm guilty. But you want to know something, he apparently taped every conversation that I had with him, but each and every time I had a conversation with him I called him from phone booths. But you see what he don't understand is that I also taped my conversations with him. So, I have them here all unedited. And when he said, "There's no note." It turns out that when he got the note from me at the art gallery, he actually ripped up a photostatic copy that I had made. Yeah, I got the original one right here for you to see!"

Wow, the head security and the museum attorney, they jumped up. When they all heard that, they fucking freaked. I had to wait and they listened to all the tapes right there and they looked at the note. I had to wait outside for the verdict and when it was over they all came out and the District Attorney said, "It was a unanimous decision. You're a free man plus you'll get back your fingerprints and an apology back from the State."

You know at the time I didn't know who the hell this guy King Tut was. I found out later on that way back then in his day, they used to wear their jewelry and they used to have these little kids holding their arms as they walked down the aisle and they used to display their jewelry. I also found out that if you have anything to do negative with King Tut you get seven years of bad luck and did I get it. That was not no bullshit. Oh man did I get it. But we'll get into that later.

Who's Better Than You!

I didn't realize it was so huge. It was 15 ounces. 15 ounces! I knew another ounce would have made it a pound. I didn't know who King Tut was. If you would have said to me, who's King Tut? I would have asked, "What is he the mayor of the Virgin Islands?

So meanwhile the ring was huge it was like carrying around a pound on your finger I wore it a couple of times and showed it to my friends. They said, 'Where the freak did you get that?' "Oh, don't worry about it. It's King Tut's ring." "Is that real?" "Yeah, it's real."

So the only one I called when I got arrested was my wife at the time. She goes, "You fucking idiot. I told you you're going to get in trouble with that ring. Why'd you do it? I said, "Oh shut the fuck up. Don't worry I'll be getting out soon." "Yeah, they're going to fucking keep you." I said, "Don't worry about it. I'll be out. I'll be out. The guy in the jewelry store was the one who purchased it."

Nobody in my family believed me. They all thought in the back of their mind, somehow we believe you got the ring, and somehow you bullshitted your way out of it. That's what they thought, especially my mother. She said, "Maybe you fool a them, but you no fool a me. I know you sell a this ring. I said, "Ma I didn't sell the ring." "No bullshit a me. You talk a nice. I think they on drugs too."

King Tut's Ring

My father, he didn't know what to think. He said, "Vinny, tell me the truth did you sell this a ring?" I said, "Pa, now do I look like I would do something like that?" He said, "Yeah." I said, "But I didn't." He said, "I know you lie good. I hope you get out of this, because this is not like Robert F. Kennedy Jr.'s dog. You have these people they send you to a Sing a Sing." He said, "You better leave everything alone. You open up the can of worms and they're going to get a you and you're going to fuck everything up. Leave it alone. Don't do nothing. Hey, you got a Sing Sing prison coming to you." I said, "Pa, don't worry." My father said, "When you say don't worry, that's when I worry."

The funny thing about it was it was when there is an event having to do with King Tut it goes nationwide and worldwide. My mother's sister called from Italy. She asked my mother, "How's your son Vinny?" My mother said to her sister, "Why you calling from over there and want to know about Vinny? I have seven kids. You only ask about one." My aunt said, "I don't know, I read something over here in the newspaper, he had a ring from somebody."

My brother Louie from California called and said, "Ma, is Vinny all right?" This was when my mother didn't know anything yet. I didn't tell her nothing for a couple of days. Everybody, my sister from Boston, my brother Frankie from

Pennsylvania was calling up. Frankie was so funny. He had this art gallery and auction place. Someone said to him, "Hey Frank is this your brother? He said, "No I have no brother, I have no relatives in New York. All my relatives are from the Midwest."

I didn't do anything. All I did was, I just tried to return it. They padlocked Ziad S.'s place and they checked all his jewelry out. They wanted to make sure he wasn't fencing jewelry.

After that a few weeks went by and I passed by the jewelry store. I said, "Hey Ziad you got any more jewelry?" He said, "You know you're out of your fucking mind man."

CHAPTER 50

MARGARET ANN'S FAVORITE VINNY VELLA CREDITS

Life With Vinny
https://www.youtube.com/watch?v=vhr5WDT7us8

Hey Vinny
https://vimeo.com/170715555

Vinny Vella and Martin Scorsese on 60 Minutes https://www.youtube.com/watch?v=x_CaLBQN550

The Irishman	2019	*Find Me Guilty*	2006
Veneration	2016	*Coffee and Cigarettes*	2003
Goat	2016		
The Vinny Vella Show MNN Cable	2013-2019	*Four Deadly Reasons*	2002
Kill The Irishman	2011	*Analyze That*	2002
The Red Corvette	2011	*The Sopranos*	1999-2004
The Last Gamble	2011	*Spenser: Small Vices*	1999
Sicilian Tale	2009	*Ghost Dog*	1999
		Casino	1995

Take a look at Vinny's IMDB page for a full listing of credits
https://www.imdb.com/name/nm0068633/

Who's Better Than You!

CHAPTER 51

WHO'S BETTER THAN YOU

Connie is my oldest sister, then comes Frankie and Louis who are my twin brothers, then comes Marie, then Cookie, then Vinny, then Nicky.

My parents' names were Helen and Louis. My mother was born in Naples. Her maiden name was Pagliarullo. My father was actually born here on Hester Street but after he was nine months old, his mother took him back to Italy. So he went to live in Bari and he came back to the United States when he was 17. So he was actually a U.S. citizen.

In later years when I went over to my mother's house, she was losing it a little bit, I would ask her, "Ma sai chi sono? (Do you know who I am?) and she said, "You are Marie," my sister's name. So, I figured if I put on lipstick she might have called me Vinny.

When I had money I would take my friends to dinner and drink. I would bring my friends along. When you are broke and have no money you start to realize who your friends are.

Who's Better Than You!

For all you people out there today that's doing these drugs, especially the ones doing cocaine today. When it comes to party time at night you go out and dance. The come down is miserable and you always want more. You want this, you want that. It's a rotten come down and you want to know something, it's really no good for you. You're just going to ruin yourself because on the cocaine it ends up on how much you are taking. It becomes hard for you to work, and hard for you to function on it. It costs a lot of money. You're wasting all your money on this stuff. You know what, you want to get high I'll tell you what to do. Listen to Vinny. If you're a guy get yourself a nice girl, if you're a girl get yourself a nice guy. Go buy a good couple of drinks, smoke a joint, you get a little buzz. You don't need to get all freaked out on cocaine, or snortin' this and taking pills. You don't need any of that. I'm not encouraging you to even smoke pot. Just go out and have a couple of drinks with your mate. That's what I do now.

I'm pretty fortunate for everything that I have and I enjoy everything that I'm doing, my movies and everything else.

A reporter asked me a question. She said "You are very charismatic, very good with women and all that. If you ever wanted to say something to a woman to make her feel good. What would you say to her?" I thought about it, and thought about it, and this is what I said, "I believe that every woman deserves or would appreciate a person male or female depending on which route she goes on, that could make her forget any problems she ever had."

As long as I can make people laugh, tell stories, have my friends around me and my family.

Hey, who's better than me.

Who's Better Than You!

Brothers
Anthony, Benjamin, Vinny

EPILOGUE

Vincent Frank Vella lived a life packed with humor, adventure, entertainment and comedy.

Vinny was married to Margaret Ann. Together they had one son Vincent Vella Jr.

Vinny was also a dad to Benjamin Hernandez, Anthony Hernandez, Jennifer Maloney and Lauren Vella.

From Vincent Vella Jr.

On behalf of my brothers Benjamin Anthony and myself, Vinny, I just want to acknowledge our Dad as a loving, hands-on father and grandfather.

We are forever grateful for his presence in our lives and the mark he made in our community.

He is greatly missed by us and our families and still lives on in our hearts. - **We love you Dad.**

Who's Better Than You!

From Alexis Hernandez

I am writing to honor my uncle, who was always like a father to me. His impact on my life, and the lives of those fortunate enough to know him, is beyond words. He had an extraordinary gift for making the people he loved feel incredibly important and special. His presence in my life was a source of immense joy and guidance, and to this day, I still feel his comforting influence.

I have fond memories of spending nights at his house, where we would laugh and eat snacks, creating a bond that was both deep and joyous. Even during the times when he was in treatment, his personality shined brightly. I remember being a kid, fascinated by the gloves and other items in the doctor's office. He would look around and whisper, "Hit it!" and I'd feel a thrill running through me as I mischievously collected these items, sharing a secret adventure with him.

Many of the stories in this book are ones I was lucky enough to hear directly from him. We'd be up past midnight, talking about his days in Miami, laughing so hard. Those nights are some of my most cherished memories, filled with his laughter and tales.

To know my uncle was to love him. I am forever thankful for the love, joy, and wisdom he brought into my life. His legacy lives on in the stories he shared and the love he gave so freely.

Who's better than him? Nobody

REST IN PEACE

VINCENT FRANK VELLA
FEBRUARY 11, 1947 – FEBRUARY 20, 2019

Vinny Vella's representative Erik Hoover gave this statement to the media upon his passing on February 20, 2019. Vinny had just celebrated his 72nd birthday on February 11th.

"We are saddened to report that Vinny Vella has passed and I'm sure that no one is more saddened than himself. Vinny loved life from his family to his friends and fans he was easily one of the funniest, endearing actors to have ever graced the screen. Vinny also had integrity and pride rarely seen. Arguably he was the fastest on the draw, the king of comebacks. His verbal jousting was legendary but many knew Vinny for his favorite saying, "Who's Better Than You."

I think we all can agree on the answer to that. It was you. It always was you! We miss you my boy.

Who's Better Than You!

www.ingramcontent.com/pod-product-compliance
Lightning Source LLC
Chambersburg PA
CBHW030326010526
44119CB00027B/392/J